WOR AL

WOR AL

A FANS' TRIBUTE TO ALAN SHEARER

tonto sport

www.tontopress.com

ISBN 0-9552183-3-0
978-0-9552183-3-0

A catalogue record for this book is
available from the British Library

Cover illustration by Tony O'Donnell
Colouring and lettering by Garen Ewing
Interior sketches by Tony O'Donnell

Printed & bound in Great Britain
by CPI Bath Press, Bath

Tonto Press
Blaydon on Tyne
United Kingdom
www.tontopress.com

In May 2006, as part of an initiative to encourage new writing, Tonto Press invited fans to pen tributes to Alan Shearer. Many of their contributions are included in this book.

CONTENTS

Introduction

An England hero and a Geordie legend, Alan Shearer is perhaps the nearest the modern game has ever had to a real-life Roy of the Rovers. His amazing goalscoring exploits are truly the stuff of comic book tales. To his fans he has become a genuine hero, a superhero, a Super Al.

As he wheeled away from goal, right arm raised, head slightly bowed in his trademark celebration, he was Superman ready for take-off, set to soar above the outstretched arms and adoring cheers. But Shearer always wore his underpants inside his trousers. Although he has become a genuine superhero in his Geordie Metropolis, he is held in such high esteem because of his very 'ordinariness', because he is one of us, because he is just like us – only far better at football. Unlike Superman, he is perhaps less our Man of Steel than our Man of Sheet Metal.

The 'sheet metal worker's son from Gosforth' has never strayed far from his roots. Not for him the trappings of celebrity, diamond earrings, pop star girlfriends, and tabloid front pages. He enjoys his wealth, certainly, and few would begrudge him his big houses, fast cars, horse racing investments, and international golfing trips. But remarkably, despite his football achievements and high profile, Shearer has managed to avoid the public scrutiny afforded to the likes of David Beckham or Wayne Rooney. The reason for this is most likely that he has been widely tagged as 'boring', a label he is no doubt delighted to live with as long as it affords him a measure of privacy. Why would the paparazzi camp outside Shearer's house when all they are likely to photograph is the big man creosoting his fence? Even his Newcastle United chairman once regrettably referred to him as a 'Mary Poppins' figure. Yet few who have shared a dressing room with Shearer would use the 'boring' tag – and certainly never to his face. (Few would flick bottle tops at him either – it's alleged that Keith Gillespie ended up bloodied in a Dublin gutter for that particular offence.) In fact, Shearer was regarded during his career as something of a practical joker in the dressing room. (He was famously credited with presenting a sheep's heart to Alessandro Pistone as a Christmas gift.)

But on the pitch he was deadly serious, single-minded, tough and uncompromising. And this built him a reputation as a player to be both feared and reviled by opposition fans – and some journalists. Criticism drove Shearer to retire early from the international game, with the captain taking abuse on behalf of an under-performing England side. Many of his critics came to regret their ostracising of England's best goalscorer in the lean years that followed. He was also criticised for his physical approach to the game, which was said to involve excessive fouling and overuse of the elbow. But again the stats tell the true story – Shearer was sent off only once in his long career, when the self-important Uriah Rennie claimed the Newcastle skipper's famous scalp after an innocuous challenge with Aston Villa's

Ian Taylor.

Shearer did play an aggressive and forceful game, fighting for every ball and appealing for every decision, but he could never be considered a cheat. He led by example, and never offered less than 100 percent effort. Eccentric commentator Stuart Hall once described him as leading the line, 'like a cavalier, broadsword drawn.' He was the best in the business at holding the ball up, he put in a wicked cross, and was often his side's best defender. He was a natural choice to captain Newcastle United and England. Few footballers can have been such inspiring leaders into battle.

But when you boil down the Shearer legend it all comes down to one commodity: goals. Loads of them. Shearer scored a hat-trick on his professional debut, and it was onwards and upwards from there. 206 goals for Newcastle, 173 more for Southampton and Blackburn, plus 30 for England. A total of 409 goals in 733 top-level games – that averages at better than a goal every other game.

There have been honours, too – the Premier League winners' medal picked up with Blackburn, a Football Writer's Footballer of the Year award, two

PFA Player of the Year awards, the accolade of Premier League Player of the Decade, the Freedom of the City of Newcastle upon Tyne, plus his Most Excellent Order of the British Empire... But can any honour compete with an indelible place in the record books as Newcastle United's – and the Premiership's – greatest ever goalscorer? Far and away the top scorer in Premier League history (upon retirement he had netted 75 times more than nearest rival Andy Cole), Shearer also broke the great Jackie Milburn's nigh-on 50-year-old record to become Newcastle United's greatest ever goalscorer.

Of course it's a crying shame that he never won a trophy with his hometown club. But Shearer hasn't shed any tears. 'When I was a young lad I wanted to play for Newcastle, wear the number 9 shirt and score goals,' he said on *Match of the Day*. Then, upon his retirement, Shearer told *The Sun*, 'It doesn't matter that I didn't win a trophy, because I did it my way and I lived the dream.' Cue Frank Sinatra's famous signature tune, as Shearer headed off into the sunset with his boots over his shoulder.

He has earned the enduring love and respect of hundreds of thousands of fans, and there is not a medal in the world that is worth swapping for that. The realisation that the Toon Army will never see his like again is tempered somewhat by the knowledge that Alan Shearer's involvement with Newcastle United has not entirely ended. For now he is 'Football Ambassador', but that could all change.

In *Roy of the Rovers*, Roy Race made a triumphant post-retirement return to Melchester Rovers as manager. Few would bet against Shearer doing similar with Newcastle United. He may return one day in the not-too-distant future as manager or coach, and may finally win something with the club he loves so much. In the meantime we can celebrate Alan Shearer's extraordinary playing career. Simply the best. Thanks for the memories, Wor Al.

Paul Brown, Newcastle United supporter, author, *Black & White Army: A Season Supporting the Toon*

Southampton

Famously the 'son of a sheet metal worker', Shearer's North East working class roots are key to his story. Alan was born on 13 August 1970 and grew up on a council estate in Gosforth. Alan starred for Wallsend Boys Club, and for Cramlington Juniors, before Newcastle United came knocking. Offered a trial, Alan famously volunteered to go in goal. The club rejected him. That decision would ultimately cost Newcastle £15 million. But railway worker and part-time Southampton scout Jack Hixon recognised Alan's potential and, after a trial at Gateshead Stadium, the 15-year-old was snapped up by the Saints.

Saint Alan

Alan arrived at Southampton thanks to our North East scout Jack Hixon, who spotted him playing for Wallsend Boys club and recommended him to Dave Merrington, Saints youth team coach at the time and a fellow Geordie. Despite having to be 400 miles from home, Shearer was not put off and soon settled in digs with a local family. He was quickly knocking in goals for fun in a youth team containing Rod Wallace and Matt Le Tissier.

Shearer went on to score 50 goals for the youth team and the clamour by fans to see him given a chance in the first team led to Chris Nicholl giving him a surprise starting debut against Arsenal on 9th April 1988. I was stood behind the Milton Road goal for that historic game, and Saints were not expected to get much from an improving Arsenal side. However, Alan Shearer burst into the match, scoring a hat-trick in a 4-2 win. The goals were never captured on video, so its hard to recall them in detail, but I remember his hat-trick goal happened right in front of me in the Milton End – when his first effort hit the bar, but he was on hand to score with the follow-up. At the time, he became the youngest ever player to score a hat-trick in England's top division, and his name was plastered all over the papers for the next few days.

Chris Nicholl had a habit of easing youngsters into the side slowly, so Shearer was in and out of the side for the rest of the season and didn't score another goal. With the arrival of Paul Rideout in the summer and the emergence of Matt Le Tissier and Rod Wallace, Saints had a very exciting front line for the next two seasons, especially with the great Jimmy Case pulling strings and 'looking after' the youngsters from midfield. Despite some good performances, Shearer was having trouble finding the net and was certainly not as prolific as he was for his subsequent clubs. That was possibly because he was given the role of the 'dog' up front, taking the knocks and chasing the defenders allowing the more skilful Rod Wallace and Matt Le Tissier to do their thing. Two games stick in my mind, and they were back to back in the 1989/90 season. We were away at QPR, and put in a stunning performance playing four strikers and scoring four goals and it could have easily been 10. The following Saturday, the previously unbeaten Liverpool came down to the Dell, and Shearer led the line against Hansen and Lawrenson and bullied the life out of them as Saints pulled off an astonishing 4-1 victory.

By the following season, Shearer was established as the number one striker and picked up the fans' Player of the Season award, despite only scoring four goals compared to 19 by Le Tiss. However, fans appreciated Shearer's 100 percent attitude and work rate, and that he was putting his body on the line in every game to allow 'Le God' to be able to have the space to do his magic. That summer, Shearer went to the U21 Toulon tournament and scored seven goals in four games as an out-and-out striker, and that started to attract the attention of all the big clubs who could see his potential as a goal-scorer, instead of just a target man.

In his last season for Saints, Shearer was pre-ferred up front by new boss Ian Branfoot, and the goals started to come more regularly. It was away at Sheffield Wednesday when I remember the now legendary 'Shearer, Shearer' chant started in ear-nest. Before that it was the old-hat 'Only One Alan Shearer', but the lad deserved his own chant.

Shearer went on to score 13 goals that season and it was soon apparent that Saints would struggle to keep him. Unlike Le Tiss, who was happy to stay at Saints, Alan's desire to improve himself meant he wanted the pressure of a big transfer, and it duly arrived when Blackburn offered a British record fee of £3.6 million (Man United were rumoured to have offered only £3m) and the rest is history.

The transfer sparked one of the funniest com-ments in Saints history when Ian Branfoot declared the combination of Speedie & Dixon, bought to re-place Shearer, would 'easily score more goals than Shearer' and that 'scoring goals was not Shearer's strength' Speedie & Dixon went on to score one goal between them that season and Branfoot was later sacked. Alan Shearer is quite rightly a football legend and I'm proud my club played a big part in putting him on the path to greatness and I was there to see it.

Keith Legg, Southampton fan, webmaster, *Saints Forever*, www.saintsforever.com

I remember seeing Alan as a young lad in the old West Stand at the Dell and immediately being struck by his obvious maturity and quiet confidence. To us Southerners, there was always something a bit different about this steely Geordie. He reminded me a bit of some Catherine Cookson hero, and of course he never lost touch with his roots.

In the early days he would warm the bench with Neil 'Razor' Ruddock and the odd couple would often come on together and turn the game. Although Alan could always look after himself, Neil became his self-appointed minder.

Alan has never forgotten the Saints and has returned for testimonials for the likes of Frannie Benali, Danny Wallace and, of course, Matt Le Tissier. Jason Dodd's benefit quickly descended into farce, with Matty in goal, defying Alan with a string of improbable saves. You could see Alan was determined to score against Le Tiss but he failed to do so even though the match ended up 9-8. I'm so proud that this great man who has achieved so much started his career at Southampton Football Club.

Frank Blighe, Southampton fan, Salisbury, Wiltshire

I was there on Alan's debut against Arsenal, which we won 4-2. The local paper had the headline 'Rookie Shearer to start' or something like that. Danny Wallace was not available and, short of strikers, in came Shearer. He lived up to his reputation as a sharp-shooter that's for sure. That hat-trick was awesome. The first goal was a header after about five minutes, the second was also a header on the half-hour, and then the third just after half-time took two attempts as it came off the bar first time. Alan Shearer scored relatively few goals for Southampton, but was more than just a goalscorer. He worked tirelessly for the team, and was a goal creator, as Matt Le Tissier, Rod Wallace, and Paul Rideout would no doubt tell you. A great player who most Saints fans will always hold close to their hearts, and who was a model professional who every child should try to aspire to. A LEGEND in my eyes.

Andy Sellar, Southampton fan, Southampton

Let me take you back to a cold dark March night in 1988. I had just left Southampton to work in Norwich, but returned for an emotional testimonial match for a lad called Steve Mills who had played for Saints (and England U21s) in the early 70s. Steve's career had been cut short by injury and he had what proved to be terminal cancer at the time of the game. The match was to be between Southampton FC and ex-Saints. SFC weren't performing particularly well at that time (some things don't change) and the expectation was that the class of the old boys (Keegan, Channon, Ball, Watson, Mills, Holmes etc) would be too much for the current side. As it happened, Southampton beat the old boys 10-1. One young player stood out: he was quick, strong and not at all overawed. The 17-year-old scored four that night. I remember looking at the programme, turning to my mate Paul Barden, and saying: 'I reckon that Alan Shearer will play for England one day...'

Graham Scott, Southampton supporter

Goal machine

A breakdown of Alan's 379 club career goals:

1987/88	Southampton	3 goals
1988/89	Southampton	0 goals
1989/90	Southampton	5 goals
1990/91	Southampton	14 goals
1991/92	Southampton	21 goals
1992/93	Blackburn Rovers	22 goals
1993/94	Blackburn Rovers	34 goals
1994/95	Blackburn Rovers	37 goals
1995/96	Blackburn Rovers	37 goals
1996/97	Newcastle United	28 goals

1997/98	Newcastle United	7 goals
1998/99	Newcastle United	21 goals
1999/00	Newcastle United	30 goals
2000/01	Newcastle United	7 goals
2001/02	Newcastle United	27 goals
2002/03	Newcastle United	25 goals
2003/04	Newcastle United	28 goals
2004/05	Newcastle United	19 goals
2005/06	Newcastle United	14 goals

Blackburn Rovers

In the summer of 1992, Alan signed for newly-promoted Blackburn Rovers and manager Kenny Dalglish. Having netted in his first games for South-ampton and England, he again made a stunning start – Alan scored twice on his full Blackburn debut. Over four seasons, Alan played 171 times for Rovers and hit a remarkable 130 goals, despite suffering career-threatening injuries. In 1994-95, Shearer hit 34 league goals to shoot Rovers to the Premier League championship. It was Shearer's only league champi-onship trophy, and the only major trophy won during his club career.

Alan of the Rovers

When the Shearer family first got to Blackburn, the Dalglishes were very good to them and made the young couple feel at home almost straightaway showing them all the hot spots and nice places in the city. Lainya had just had Chloe for a week and the couple were in a rented home. Marina Dalglish went out of her way to help her settle.

Alan's goal scoring record wasn't particularly good at Southampton and a lot of people questioned the amount Rovers paid for his services. On top of that a lot of fans were very disappointed to see David Speedie, who had scored the goals that got

Blackburn into the newly created Premier League, go to Southampton as part of the Shearer deal. There was a lot of pressure on Alan to do well.

But Shearer got off to a great start with his new team mates who were pleased to see he was willing to give 100 percent all the time. And once the season got under way, the Rovers fans soon had a new hero; Alan scored twice on his full debut, a 3-3 draw at Selhurst Park against Crystal Palace.

All the way to the Christmas period, Shearer scored a total of 16 league goals for his new club including five braces. Such good form made him into an England regular scoring his second international goal in a 4-0 win over Turkey in a qualifier for the 1994 World Cup.

But things came to a very sudden halt on Boxing Day 1992. Blackburn were playing Leeds at Ewood Park and were leading three goals to one. With ten minutes to go. Alan, who had already scored twice putting the game beyond the opposing side, was chasing a long ball up the pitch. He got caught in between a Leeds defender and their goalkeeper. Once the challenge was over, Shearer was left in a motionless heap just outside the penalty area –

something was wrong. He was taken off and it was later revealed he had snapped his anterior cruciate ligament in his right knee. He rested it for the following ten days, tried training, but it went once again.

Shearer missed the remainder of the season for Blackburn and England, having to watch World Cup qualifiers from home. 16 goals in the 21 games in which he did feature for the Rovers was an excellent record, the season ended sourly however, as it became clear England would fail to qualify for the World Cup. It was his very first test of character in professional football, but Alan had a great attitude and knew what the injury was, and that he would be back.

Sure enough, the following summer, Shearer was back in full training. Blackburn went to Ireland for a preseason tour and Kenny Dalglish decided it was right to include him in the squad. Alan was put on the bench and was told not to expect to be playing straight away. But with ten minutes to go in their first game of the tour, Kenny put Alan on and, despite there being so little time left, he managed to score twice.

Once the Premier League campaign got under

way, Shearer was put on the bench and only given 20 minutes as a substitute, Dalglish wanted to slowly break him in. Four games in and the main man was back on the score sheet again against Newcastle, of all teams, at St James' Park. Sure enough, two games after that Shearer was back in the starting 11.

Eventually, Shearer settled down at Blackburn and became the most feared goal scorer in the Premiership. He bagged an astounding 31 goals from 40 games in the 1993-4 season as the Rovers finished a close second in the table behind Manchester United. On top of that, Alan won the honour of Footballer of the Year for that season. He added three more goals to his England tally as well.

In the summer that followed, Blackburn signed young striker Chris Sutton for £5 million from Norwich City. Shearer continued from where he had left off the previous campaign, and with Sutton formed a deadly partnership that was known as the SAS. From 42 games, Alan scored a phenomenal 34 goals. In the previous season, Blackburn had always been chasing behind Man United, but this time around they were top of the league from November onwards. They should probably have sealed the Premier League title with five or six games to go, but as Blackburn hadn't won anything for a long time, the pressure got to the players. And everything came down to the last day of the season.

After 42 league games, Blackburn Rovers were deservedly crowned Premiership champions but it was after a final day scare, an emotional final day full of drama for the East Lancashire club. Blackburn were away at Anfield to play Liverpool while Manchester United were to play West Ham at Upton Park. Man United's nerves had started to show in midweek, when they needed a late Denis Irwin penalty to beat Southampton and ensure that the title race went to the wire. Man United needed a win on the final day of the season in order to overtake Rovers.

Alan Shearer provided the first twist in the tale that day, putting Rovers 1-0 up from a Stuart Ripley low cross on 20 minutes. That event was briefly followed at Upton Park, although it was the Hammers who earned a shock lead as Michael Hughes finished to put the Red Devils temporarily out of the title picture to universal acclaim at Anfield, the Liverpudlians applauding at the prospect of their rivals failing to retain their hold on the championship. At the break, Rovers were in full control, but things would quickly change.

Brian McClair squeezed in an early second half equaliser for Man United, and on 64 minutes an equaliser came at Anfield too as John Barnes put the home side level. Nerves started to show on Merseyside and in East London as both title contenders missed golden opportunities to take the lead. As time was running out, the news came in that Man United, despite all their efforts had failed to beat the Hammers. Jamie Redknapp even curled in a late winner for Liverpool, but even though Blackburn had lost this battle, they had won the war. Unbelievable scenes followed on Merseyside as players hugged each other as the game continued and Kenny Dalglish was congratulated by Scousers all around.

An emotional Jack Walker was standing proud with a tear in his eye applauding his heroes. The team that Jack built had pulled off a great achievement and were champions of England. To the Premiership crown, Alan added the personal honours of top goal scorer and PFA Player of the Year for the

1994-5 campaign.

The next season, expectations were very high for Rovers to do well and it was hard for the team to live up to them. They simply didn't win enough league or cup games in the first months of the season to be in contention again. Their Champions League campaign was a disappointment too, as they got knocked out in the group stages. The team pulled their socks up and played some great football from December onwards and rose up the table with only two other teams doing better. On a personal level, Alan won the golden boot once again scoring 31 goals in 35 games (including four hat-tricks) making him the first player to score 30-plus goals in three consecutive seasons.

After a great Euro 96, Alan had become one of the most famous strikers in the world. He finished top scorer in the tournament spearheading England to the semi finals. In all eight different clubs made inquiries for Alan that summer, Manchester United, Liverpool, Arsenal, Everton, Newcastle, Internazionale, Juventus and Barcelona. The foreign clubs were soon put aside, as Alan wanted to stay in England. Advanced talks took place with Alex Ferguson, and

Alan was close to signing for Man United.

Jack Walker had put a price tag on Alan – he couldn't leave Rovers for a penny less than £15 million! Newcastle United, the club he had supported all his life, managed to come up with the fee and Blackburn Rovers just couldn't turn it down.

As for what came next – ten years have gone by so quickly yet it seems so much has happened. At the end of the day, it doesn't really matter whether Shearer, the Newcastle United player, won anything or not during his tenure up North, he has been an inspiration to so many on and off the pitch and has left us with enough memories to last a life time. Of course an FA Cup here and there would probably not have gone amiss, but at the same time it is a great lesson for us all to learn – that life isn't always a fairytale. I for one feel privileged to have been able to follow his career.

Matthew Koziol, Alan Shearer fansite webmaster, *Shearer 9*, www.shearer9.com

What to me speaks most clearly about how highly-respected Alan Shearer is was the ovation he received this year at Blackburn, when, in Newcastle colours, he returned for his final competitive match at Ewood Park. It's extremely rare to see a visiting player get such a warm reception from the home crowd, and it was truly a heart-warming moment.

Matthew Darwin, Blackburn Rovers fan

The signing of Alan Shearer was unbelievable. The man was Mr Blackburn Rovers from day one. How could anyone who went to the first Premiership game at Palace forget two of the most remarkable debut goals that will ever be seen? At Blackburn we saw the man at his very best, and a player who epitomised the good old-fashioned striker. Thanks Alan for some of the most marvellous memories, as Rovers fans we lived the dream because of two men: Jack Walker and you. You did us proud, as you have Newcastle and England. You deserve your place in history as England's greatest ever centre forward.

Warren Gibson, Blackburn fan, Leyland, Lancashire

Premier class

FA Premier League top goalscorers to May 06:

1	**Alan Shearer**	260 goals
2	Andrew Cole	185 goals
3	Thierry Henry	164 goals
4	Robbie Fowler	159 goals
5	Les Ferdinand	149 goals
6	Teddy Sheringham	145 goals
7	Jimmy Floyd Hasselbaink	126 goals
8	Michael Owen	125 goals
9	Dwight Yorke	122 goals
10	Ian Wright	113 goals

FA Premier League top scorers in a season:

1= **Alan Shearer** (Blackburn, 1994-95) 34 goals

1= Andrew Cole (Newcastle, 1993-94) 34 goals

FA Premier League top scorers in a match:

1= **Alan Shearer** (Newcastle United) 5 goals
Newcastle United vs Sheff Wednesday (19/09/1999)

1= Andrew Cole (Manchester United) 5 goals
Manchester United vs Ipswich Town (04/03/1995)

FA Premier League Golden Boot winner:

1994–95 **Alan Shearer** (Blackburn Rovers) 34 goals

1995–96 **Alan Shearer** (Blackburn Rovers) 31 goals

1996–97 **Alan Shearer** (Newcastle United) 25 goals

FA Premier League Player of the Decade:

1992–2002 **Alan Shearer** (Blackburn & Newcastle)

England

Alan made his England debut while at Southampton in 1992 – scoring in a 2-0 friendly win over France. He went on to play 63 games and score 30 goals for his country. He also had the honour of captaining England on 31 occasions. Alan spearheaded his country's campaigns at the 1998 World Cup Finals, and the 1996 and 2000 European Championships. He retired from international football in 2000 as England's sixth highest ever goalscorer.

England's number one

France had gone 19 games undefeated when they came to Wembley to face England in a friendly on 19 February 1992. This game was important for a number of reasons: We won, the then 20-year-old Alan Shearer made his England debut... and he scored.

'Geoff Thomas took a corner and Mark Wright headed it down to me,' reminisced Shearer. 'I had my back to goal, but I swivelled and hit it and the next thing I knew it was in the back of the net.'

The hand was raised and the now famous Shearer celebration heralded the first of many international goals.

Shearer's first real chance to impress at the highest level came at the 1996 European Champion- ships, after England failed to qualify for the 1994 World Cup. He'd gone 12 games without scoring for his country, although in the same space of time, had managed over 60 goals for his club. Everyone was wondering whether he'd score for England ever again and while every man and his dog seemed to be criti- cising Shearer's ability, Venables kept the faith.

We kicked off the Euro 96 opener at Wembley against Switzerland, firm favourites to win. Why didn't anyone tell that to the team? They were tense and anxious and lacked inspiration. In short, we were a team that was never going to create any opportunities... until, out of the blue, Paul Ince played a perfect through ball that big Al latched on to and banged into the back of the net. The doubters were silenced – temporarily. Inevitably, Switzerland eventually won a penalty and equalised. It may have been a draw, but Alan had broken his duck and was spared by the critics as the rest of the team were slated in the press.

A victory in the following game against Scotland was crucial. The first half ended goal-less, but

Shearer stood up to be counted. After the break, young full back Gary Neville floated a cross over to the far post; Alan stooped low and got onto the end of it, netting another. England went on to win 2-0 in a famous victory helped on the way by an important penalty save by David Seaman and a classic goal by Paul Gascoigne. With the press and the fans back on the team's side, the whole nation started to believe their team could go all the way, 30 years after the 1966 World Cup.

The Dutch were up next, a side not to be under-estimated. What happened that day in the Wembley sunshine of June 18th 1996 will live long in England fans' memories. England dominated proceedings from the whistle, playing them off the park in a 4-1 thrashing. On 23 minutes, Ince was brought down by Dutch defender Danny Blind in the penalty area and up stepped Mr Alan Shearer to score his third goal in as many games. Sheringham made it 2-0 after the break and set Shearer up for a classic collective goal. The ball went from McManaman to Gascoigne to Sheringham to Shearer, who hit it first time past a helpless Van der Sar. There was no denying he'd found his form – cue Shear Magic headlines – and a goal drought becoming a flood. Sheringham added another before Kluivert reduced the deficit.

The strike force was brought off by Venables to rapturous applause, and emotional renditions of *Three Lions* rang out over the pitch as fans paid tribute to our heroes. Shearer and Sheringham had arguably their greatest game as a partnership and England finished top of their group. With four goals in three games, Alan was now attracting attention to himself from all over the globe. Word was out. England had a new King.

In the quarter finals, Spain held their own and we were somewhat outplayed. The game went all the way to a penalty shootout; the first one England had been involved in since that infamous night in Italy back in 1990. First to step up was Shearer, putting his shot past Zubizarreta with ease. Seaman eventually saved Nadal's strike to send England into the semis.

England versus Germany was a game worthy of the final, but only one of the two sides would advance. Shearer gave England the perfect start when he headed them in front after three minutes from a well-worked corner kick. Just like against the Swiss, their early goal unsettled England more than their opponents and in the 16th minute, Kuntz equalised, and it went to penalties once again.

Alan stepped up first this time too, and his spot kick finished the same way his other two of the tournament did... right in the back of the net. The dream ended when Southgate blundered, but Shearer was the Euro 96 top scorer with five goals in five matches and was now the most feared striker in Europe as a result. Golden Boot to Wor Al, that'll do nicely, thank you.

Euro 96 was the turning point in his career, putting his name on the international scene as one of the best strikers in the business. There wasn't a club anywhere on earth that didn't want him on their side. But only a few could actually afford him.

Four years later it was a different story: Euro 2000, with Shearer on board as skipper in Kevin Keegan's team. England were the underdogs and fans wanted Owen, not Shearer, claimed one newspaper headline, saying, 'Most England fans believe captain Alan Shearer should be left out of Kevin Keegan's starting line-up for Euro 2000, according to a new poll.'

53 minutes into the match, Shearer headed home the only goal of the game, courtesy of a David Beckham cross. Poll schmoll... Shearer had saved England's skin, but had finally taken all he could from the critics. England lost 3-2 to Romania three days later, and, although he'd proved his worth again, Shearer quit international football following the tournament.

Stuart Wheatman, Newcastle fan, author, *The Krays: The Geordie Connection*

30 goals

A rundown of Alan's 30 England goals:

1	19/02/1992	FR	FRANCE	2-0
2	18/11/1992	WQ	TURKEY	4-0
3	17/05/1994	FR	GREECE	5-0
4	07/09/1994	FR	USA	2-0
5	07/09/1994	FR	USA	2-0
6	08/06/1996	EC	SWITZERLAND	1-1
7	15/06/1996	EC	SCOTLAND	2-0
8	18/06/1996	EC	NETHERLANDS	4-1
9	18/06/1996	EC	NETHERLANDS	4-1
10	26/06/1996	EC	GERMANY	1-1

11	01/09/1996 WQ	MOLDOVA	3-0
12	09/10/1996 WQ	POLAND	2-1
13	09/10/1996 WQ	POLAND	2-1
14	30/04/1997 WQ	GEORGIA	2-0
15	31/05/1997 WQ	POLAND	2-0
16	07/06/1997 FR	FRANCE	1-0
17	22/04/1998 FR	PORTUGAL	3-0
18	22/04/1998 FR	PORTUGAL	3-0
19	15/06/1998 WC	TUNISIA	2-0
20	30/06/1998 WC	ARGENTINA	2-2
21	05/09/1998 EQ	SWEDEN	1-2
22	14/10/1998 EQ	LUXEMBOURG	3-0
23	28/04/1999 FR	HUNGARY	1-1
24	09/06/1999 EQ	BULGARIA	1-1
25	04/09/1999 EQ	LUXEMBOURG	6-0
26	04/09/1999 EQ	LUXEMBOURG	6-0
27	04/09/1999 EQ	LUXEMBOURG	6-0
28	10/10/1999 FR	BELGIUM	2-1
29	17/06/2000 EC	GERMANY	1-0
30	20/06/2000 EC	ROMANIA	2-3

Newcastle United

In *1996, after excelling for England at the European Championships, Alan left Blackburn Rovers – and it seemed he would join Manchester United. But instead, seemingly at the last moment, Alan signed for Kevin Keegan's Newcastle United in a record-breaking £15 million deal. 15,000 fans descended on St James' Park to welcome their new hero. 'I hope I can spend the rest of my career here,' Alan told them. 'It is a dream come true.' Ten years and 206 goals later... the rest is history.*

Shearer's coming home

Was it one of those JFK moments? Can you remember where you were when Big Al signed? Funnily enough I can, although the mists of time have long since erased the exact date from my memory.

But I do remember being at home during the week, which was unusual, and even more unusually I had the TV on. It must have been fate and destiny as the breaking news came on that Alan Shearer had just signed for Newcastle.

I had to listen again, was England's Captain and centre-forward really coming home to play for his beloved Newcastle? Had King Kev finally pulled off the biggest transfer coup of all, and let's face it he pulled off a lot! Yes, he had, and it was true but it took me some time to persuade my mate at work as I immediately phoned him and gave him the news.

I felt quite privileged as I talked on the phone outlining the deal to my mate as I could here numerous other phones in the office going off as the rest of the world came to terms with the record transfer. I also remember at the time that not one of us mentioned the fee. It didn't matter. Shearer was coming home to a team and club going places, and was surely the final piece of the jigsaw that would see numerous trophies and glory follow.

Fast forward ten years and something did go wrong because despite Big Al's efforts those trophies did not arrive and ultimately, whatever he says, I guess there will always be a regret that he didn't deliver the long awaited silverware. But, that's where I stop being negative as no one will ever believe that Shearer was at any way at fault for that. Throughout his time at Newcastle he has been simply magnificent and if trophies had followed no one in football would have begrudged them.

However, I also believe that if you asked any Newcastle fan if they would swap a trophy for not having had ten years of Shearer then I think you'd find the vast majority answering no! Quite simply us Geordies love a No 9, and if he's local all the better!

Shearer has said he has no regrets, Freddie Shepherd has no regrets about signing him, and the fans have had no regrets having had him in their side. The respect, admiration and adulation he has received from the Geordie public has been heartfelt and genuine. His love for the club, city and fans is unquestionable as he's stretched every sinew in his undying desire to do well for all and sundry.

We have appreciated every one of his efforts and know that no one could have done more for his hometown club. He's led from the front in more ways than one and his tenure at the Toon has been fantastic. No one could have given more and tried harder. The Geordies know and respect that and that's one of many reasons he's so revered.

So what about personal highlights from his ten years? Gosh, there are so many! The home debut against Wimbledon when he lined that free-kick up and you knew he would score. The hat-trick against Leicester in the last ten minutes or so to turn a 3 – 1 defeat in to a 4 – 3 win. His two performances and goals in the semi-finals of the FA Cup that at least meant we went to two finals.

Goals at the Gallowgate End against Everton, Chelsea and Aston Villa were all stunners and up there with some of the best I've ever seen. His part in the 5-0 drubbing of Man United when he re-confirmed that if he hadn't made it as a centre-forward he might have made it as a winger. His partnerships with Sir Les and Craig Bellamy – won-derful combinations that brought great times and so much pleasure. Goals in Europe that showed the rest of the continent that he could score in whatever competition he played in. Quite simply there are so many memories I could fill a book myself! But there are three things I'd like to finish with.

Firstly, his last goal was in a Tyne/Wear derby. It may have only been a penalty but as the man himself said, 'If that's how I go out then it's not a bad way to finish'. And he also showed how much those games meant to him be reminding everyone that it was a goal he was owed after a previous pen-alty miss against the same opposition.

Secondly, every time he got the ball in the box he worked the goalkeeper. You knew that it would either be a goal or a save. Only very rarely did he miss the target.

Thirdly, we have not seen the last of him at Newcastle. His love for the club is legendary, and I won't be alone in believing whatever role he takes on he'll be a success. He's a born winner and a hard worker and the two things merged usually mean success.

So, thank you Alan Shearer for ten wonderful years and many magical memories. Whatever the future holds and brings you'll always have a place in our hearts.

Jeff King, lifelong Newcastle United supporter, Cramlington

Simply the best

Newcastle United's all-time top goalscorers:

1	Alan Shearer	1996-06	206 goals
2	Jackie Milburn	1946-57	200 goals
3	Len White	1953-62	153 goals
4	Hughie Gallacher	1925-30	143 goals
5	Malcolm MacDonald	1971-76	121 goals
6	Peter Beardsley	1983-97	119 goals
7=	Bobby Mitchell	1949-61	113 goals
7=	Tom McDonald	1921-31	113 goals
9	Neil Harris	1920-25	101 goals
10	Bryan 'Pop' Robson	1962-71	97 goals

A sheet-metal worker's son from Gosforth

It sounds silly now, but I'd better get an admission out of the way right at the start: when Kevin Keegan brought Alan Shearer home from Blackburn Rovers in July 1996, smashing the club record transfer fee in the process, I was unconvinced. After all (as I remember telling anyone down the pub who would listen) if it was a swashbuckling number 9 in the English tradition we were looking for, didn't we already have one in Les Ferdinand, whose 29 goals in the season just ended had brought us so close to that elusive Premiership title? If Kevin had £15 million to spend, surely he was better off splashing out on a couple of trusty centre-halves to shore up that infamous leaky defence?

This scepticism over the wisdom of Keegan's eye-catching swoop put me in a minority of one among my friends, who rolled their eyes in barely-concealed derision – and a couple of days later the scenes which greeted the unveiling of the new number 9 on the steps of St James' Park proved that Shearermania had truly taken hold among the Geordie faithful at large. As the sun blazed down, stadium MC Alan Robson, narrowly avoiding being upstaged by two giant inflatable Brown Ale bottles standing sentry-like at his shoulders, presided over scenes of near-hysteria, and 'Wor Alan', as we were already learning to call him, took the microphone to remind us that at heart he was just one of us – 'a sheet-metal worker's son from Gosforth'.

August came, and the stage-managed razzmatazz on the stadium steps gave way to serious action on the pitch. The prodigal centre-forward opened his St James' account with the second of two goals against Wimbledon, sealing the first win of the season. By late September, a trademark snapshot from the edge of the eighteen-yard box was enough to secure victory at Elland Road, and lift us to top spot in the League for the first time since the traumatic denouement of the previous campaign. As the nights began to close in, even a sceptic like me was start-ing to get carried along by the excitement. It really did seem as though Shearer was ready to lead us to the Promised Land.

We never quite got there, of course. That first 1996-97 season, when we finished second again, was the nearest in the Shearer era that we ever came to bringing home the ultimate prize. But, hell, we had a bloody good go for glory during those ten years – along the way sharing some memorable days and nights. For me, the one that stands out was a midweek cup-tie at Blackburn in January 2000. It is a game that has come to sum up for me what Alan Shearer – the player, and the man – is all about.

In the run-up to the game, excitement on Tyne-side was running high. In the previous rounds we had made short work of Tottenham Hotspur and Sheffield United, so a fifth-round away tie at Pre-miership Blackburn held no fears. Among the eight thousand Geordies who made the journey down to

Lancashire that Wednesday night, the feeling was that our name was on the cup.

Mind you I was lucky to be there at all. The away allocation having been sold out within days, I had scammed my way to a home-end seat courtesy of the Blackburn ticket office, with the aid of a dodgy put-on Lancashire accent and no little amount of persistence. I took up my place along the touchline among what I took to be home supporters; the plan was to watch in silence while transmitting my support for the Magpies through carefully directed telepathy. Unfortunately, just as I was sending an urgent brainwave message to the nearby Robert Lee, Shearer scored the opening goal, and my well-laid plans went right out of the window.

I couldn't contain myself, and responded to Wor Alan's low drive past the hapless keeper in Gallowgate End fashion – launching myself four feet in the air and landing on a bloke in the row in front. On my way down there was plenty of time to anticipate what would surely be a sound beating at the hands of these strange, mute Lancastrians whose company I had so rudely infiltrated – but I needn't have worried. My companions in the stand turned out, of course, to be fellow Geordies. Shearer's goal had unmasked us – and as the game wore on, all subterfuge was dropped. By the end, we were joining in wholeheartedly with 'The Blaydon Races' being belted out by the seven thousand 'bona-fide' away fans to our right.

By this time we had plenty to sing about. Seemingly galvanised by the 'Judas' taunts of the Blackburn fans, Shearer had given a classic demonstration of the English centre-forward's art. That opening goal was quickly equalised, but it seemed only a matter of time before the visitors forged ahead once more- and sure enough, Shearer was on hand to slam home a rising 70th minute winner from close-range, before, in a surprising departure from that understated one-arm salute we had come to know and love, sliding behind the goal on his backside to take the acclaim of a Darwen End lost in rapture. Our passage to the quarter finals having been secured, surely nobody could stop us now.

Of course, in the semi-finals we would see that Chelsea could, would, and did. But for those two glorious hours at Ewood Park, standing and singing among undercover comrades from among a travelling Geordie Army numbering nearly ten thousand, I really did believe Shearer was leading us towards silverware. It wasn't to be, but despite all those cruel late-season moments when glory was snatched away from us, I for one am glad to have been around to see him try. In fact you know what – I have changed my mind. Perhaps the signing of Alan Shearer was not such a terrible idea, after all.

Jonathan Baker, Newcastle supporter for 20 years, Manchester, http://crinklybee.typepad.com/

The day we caught the train

I was standing at a train station, on a monumental excursion from Amsterdam to Plymouth, via Rotterdam, Hull and York – which was where it happened. There was this guy down the platform, idly working his way through a broadsheet crossword and, although I thought I knew him, I just couldn't put my finger on who he was.

Initially, I'd gone on one of those '40 minutes to kill' excursions that usually incorporates a good look through the papers in WH Smiths, a meaningless rifle through timetables and leaflets in the ticket office and an overpriced beaker of something masquerading as tea.

My partner Kelly – who is now my wife and whose parents live in the West Country (hence the visit to Plymouth), had sensibly opted to stay put in the waiting room with a trashy magazine for company. As such, with said trash occupying her every thought, I decided to seek outside help in the shape of my (half) brother, Dan (same name, long story).

I headed for the nearest payphone (remember them?) and dialled my home number in North Shields, where my brother was staying whilst we were away. It was a warm July weekday and, unbeknown to me at this point, the kind of close-season lunchtime that any self-confessed football fan would walk a million miles for. The conversation went something like this:

Payphone: Brrrrr brrrrr. Brrrrr brrrrr. Brrrr b - click
Dan (sounding louder than normal and slightly out of breath): Hello...
Me: Alright Dan mate, it's me.
Dan: (Shouting) DAN... DAN, BLOODY HELL DAN, WHERE ARE YOU?
Me: Erm, I'm in York – listen, what was the name of

that guy – the one out of that mushy film with the Scouse woman in it? I think he's Scottish?

Dan: WHAT??

Me: You know, man, he was in that film with Bowie years ago.

Dan (bewildered): What? Who the... WHAT YOU ON ABOUT?

Me: I think he might have been in *Local Hero* too.

Dan (obviously preoccupied but never one to miss out on a bit of banal trivia): Denis Lawson? The pilot bloke out of Star Wars?

Me: Na – not him. What was that film called – set in Greece? Ah forget it – anyway, how are you?

Dan: How am... DAN, MAN, HAVE YOU NOT HEARD?

Me: Heard what?

Dan: SHEARER, MAN – ALAN SHEARER. ALAN BLOODY SHEARER!

Me (calm but confused): What about him?

Dan (laughing nervously and trying to talk/shout all at once): What abou... HE'S SIGNED MAN – HE'S OURS! 15 MILLION QUID!

At this point, two things happened. My initial reaction was to scream out loud, run around York station like some sort of frenzied child and actively seek out Man United fans to go 'aaaaaggggghhhhhh' at. Quite a natural, mature and measured response, I'm sure you'll agree.

My second, and simultaneous thought was one of trepidation – a natural emotion triggered by 26 years of following Newcastle United and all that that has entailed.

The cynical Geordie realism department of my brain – a section which had been fuelled and stoked to its limit some months earlier thanks to our inglorious collapse in the title run-in of 95/96, kicked into action. How can we have signed Alan Shearer? £15 million? But that's like, a world record?

I might add that, in the hours and days previous to this point in time, we had been out of the country and doing that typically British thing of scouring foreign shops for signs of a familiar masthead – The Mirror, The Guardian – hell, even The Star would do.

On one occasion, after I'd managed to locate one of the above, some mischievous designer had even mocked up a Panini sticker style image of what Shearer might look like in his spanking new Man U kit.

Then on the ferry back to Hull, there was one of those squabbling groups of 12-year-old footballers on their way back from a friendly tournament in the Netherlands – all with Yorkshire accents and almost all bearing some kind of Manchester United apparel about their person.

As we sat at the bar, resplendent in our grand-dad-collared Brown Ale Toon shirts, they goaded us – much to the embarrassment of their embittered, Leeds-supporting guardians. 'Where's your trophy gone?' laughed one, referring to the previous seasons monumental cave-in. 'Shearer, Shearer, Shearer!' chanted a handful of others – utterly convinced that England's fully-evolved hero of Euro 96 was on his way to Old Trafford.

And I suppose the reason I was so torn upon hearing my brother's claims was that, I too was convinced. In any case, why would he come to Newcastle? Sure he's from Gosforth, his family probably all live there and he'd be worshiped by every Geordie in the world but, in my experience, that was never a good enough reason for Waddle, Beardsley and Gascoigne to stick around when a so-called bigger club came calling – why should Shearer be any different?

With my in-built caution on full alert, the conversation resumed.

Me: That's great Dan – where did you hear this? The tabloids? Oh no, let me guess, The Sun right? It must be true then.

Dan: WHAT? What you on about? It's on, man, it's true – it's all over The Chronicle – everyone's going mad. HE'S OURS!

Me: The Chronicle?

Dan: Aye – FRONT PAGE!

Me (slight change of tone): What – really?

Dan: YEAH, listen (reads out the opening couple of paragraphs)...SEE – He's signed, man. THIS IS IT!

A silence descended on me as six trillion thoughts all rushed through my head at once: 'The Chronicle wouldn't splash on this if it wasn't true would they?', '15 million – that's big-time money' and 'I thought he was practically a Man U player' until the process lead me to a joyful conclusion. 'Blimey – IT MUST BE TRUE!'

Our phone conversation then erupted into hysterical laughter interspersed with hollers of 'I don't believe it' and the odd, ever cautious 'you're not kidding me are you, Dan boy?' from me.

Hysteria began its decent into fervent and enthusiastic banter along the lines of 'Shearer and Ferdinand – amazing' and 'There's no stopping us now man' with 'I don't believe it' always within touching distance.

Then, abruptly, the pips went. We had days worth of fresh, Toon-related dialogue on our hands and we had to cram it into five seconds. It ended 'I'll give you a ring late...' click, brrrrrrrrrrrrrr.

And there I was – loaded with the kind of news I'd only ever dreamt of. My team – Newcastle United, had signed arguably the best striker in the world, for a world-record fee, and while all of Tyneside was awash with a verbal and tangible clatter of excitement, I was in bloody York.

I half walked, half ran back to the news stands of WH Smith's, which I'd obliviously thumbed through earlier. I was eagerly scanning the racks for York's equivalent of the Evening Chronicle when I spotted a bound pile of newspapers yet to be displayed. And there it was.

It was only small, a kind of 'news in brief' piece

but on the front page, but its headline was all I needed. It read something like 'Newcastle Land Shearer in Record Deal' and, as I stood there, on a random train station amidst the unlikeliest of journeys, the world might as well of stopped all together. It was real.

In the immediate aftermath I remembered we had a train to catch, and I wandered, dazed and almost laughing to myself, back to the waiting room where the uninformed Kelly was, well, waiting.

'What's wrong with you?' she inquired, as I stumbled through the door. 'You look...weird.'

'I'm fine,' I said, sitting down next to her. 'It's just that Newcastle have signed Alan Shearer for 15 million pounds.'

'Really,' she replied, in an alarmingly nonplussed manner. 'I've just seen Tom Conti doing a crossword.'

Dan Sheridan, football writer and Newcastle United season ticket holder, Cullercoats

One of our own

It's difficult to know how to describe the career of our most prolific number 9. I remember waking up, turning on the TV and hearing the news that Alan Shearer was signing for us back in 1996. I remember the feeling of excitement that coursed through my veins – this was the big one, we'd broken the world record to sign the best striker available, and he was a Geordie (a sheet metal worker's son from Gosforth, as he kept reminding us).

Things started brightly, with Shearer and Les Ferdinand forging a formidable partnership up front. At the time, both had pace and power and must have been a defender's nightmare. That both were been a defender's nightmare. That both were on the score-sheet as we annihilated Manchester United 5-0 showed that it was a partnership in the true sense of the word.

Unfortunately, Keegan's departure in January 1997, after we had demolished Spurs 7-1 (two a piece for Alan and Les) heralded a new era at St James Park. Sadly these were dark times as Kenny Dalglish disbanded the team that had almost won the league, selling Ferdinand in the process, failed to rebuild it so that it came anywhere close to emulating Keegan's side and we never again looked like challenging for the league title, despite having Shearer in our midst. His goals might have taken us to FA Cup finals at Wembley twice (once under Dalglish and once under Ruud Gullitt), but on both occasions we froze on the big stage, and were outplayed by better sides.

For Shearer things seemed to go from bad to worse – Gullitt's strong opinions and lack of faith in the striker meant Shearer was forced to change his game, and in doing so he became less effective. The nadir of that particular time came during a home game against Sunderland when young striker Paul

Robinson took Shearer's place in the starting eleven. Perhaps unsurprisingly, we lost, and that defeat saw the Dutchman shown the door, heralding a new era under Bobby Robson.

Robson, who many had touted for the job when Keegan left, had an immediate impact on Shearer – and his astute advice saw Shearer return to form with a vengeance, hammering five past Sheffield Wednesday in Robson's second game in charge. Shearer went on to score 30 goals in all competitions for the club that season.

As the years progressed and we proved incapable of building a team strong enough to challenge for the league title, the UEFA Cup held out the hand of hope, only to cruelly snatch away the prospect of a trophy as we capitulated on foreign soil, and age and injury ravaged our once great striker.

Despite all that though, Shearer will always remain a legend as a player for Newcastle. As a supporter, Shearer achieved the things that I wanted to do (and would have done, but for a lack of talent). He's scored goals for, and captained Newcastle United Football Club, and he's done it with such regularity that he's now the club's all-time leading goalscorer.

The thing that marks Shearer out as special is that he's one of us. He might be a multi-millionaire footballer, who once commanded a world record transfer fee, who scored 30 goals in 63 games for England, whose goals won the league title for Blackburn Rovers, but beyond all that he's still someone who grew up supporting Newcastle United. Like each and every one of us, you know he'd give blood for the cause and play through the pain barrier if it meant the difference between winning and losing.

For 99.99 percent of us, it will always remain an unfulfilled dream to run out at St James Park in the black and white shirt, while 52,000 chant your name. But, if we can't go out and score goals for Newcastle, what better than for one of our own to do it for us, someone who knows just what it means to watch the ball crash into the Gallowgate net?

I'd have liked it to have been me, but it wasn't, it was him and he's done a outstanding job as my deputy, and for that I will always remember him fondly.

Paul Wakefield, Newcastle season ticket holder, www.blackandwhiteandreadallover.blogspot.com

There are many great memories of Alan Shearer that come to mind, but for me the one I will never forget is the day Shearer was presented to his beloved Toon Army on the 6th August 1996. Everyone had known for a few weeks that he was signing but that day confirmed he was back where he belonged, he came home! Over 15,000 fans turned up to greet him outside the steps of St James' and the atmosphere was electric. He stepped up onto the podium and the place went wild. Keegan said he was 'the signing for all the Geordie people'. We had just missed out on the title the previous season but after signing Shearer I felt at last we could win something. Alas it wasn't to be, but he did score in the 5-0 rout of Man Utd in that first season and I think he loved that goal just as much as we did. If only the signings that have come and gone in the ten years Shearer has been at the club showed half the commitment and dedication he has given us, we may have had a cabinet full of trophies. Aal the best Al, enjoy your retirement, you deserve it.

David Lynn, season ticket holder, North Shields

I was on my way back from a driving holiday in France, and my girlfriend was at the wheel of our open-topped car as we headed up the M1. My mobile phone rang and it was my old school friend Micky on the line. He said, simply, 'Si, we've got him!' and he then began to laugh hysterically. Although there had been no mention of a name, and despite the fact we'd never discussed any speculation prior to this, I replied only with, 'How much?' Micky said, 'Fifteen million.' That was the end of one of the most memorable conversations of my life. I could bleat on forever about the joy Alan has brought to us all, but I think my favourite quote is from Sky TV's coverage of the 5-0 win over Manchester United, in which Martin Tyler said, 'Beardsley!... It's another one!... No! Ferdinand!... Shearer!... Of course!' Special times.

Simon Donald, Newcastle United supporter

A dream signing

I can remember the day Shearer signed like it was yesterday. We were on a family holiday in Newquay, and in between visiting the local A&E with minor ailments and shivering under the protection of beach towels and windbreaks, we decided to have a walk down the local high street. While fighting past the huge amounts of overweight surfer wannabes in Fat Willy's t-shirts we passed a Dixon's store. What we saw through its window left us stunned. *Football Focus* was on the muted television, and a picture of a serious looking Alan Shearer sat in a square in the centre of the screen with four wonderful words underneath: ALAN SHEARER NEWCASTLE UNITED. Was this some kind of joke? Was it just a rumour? We needed details, and I considered buying the telly there and then to find out more. But then the picture of Shearer disappeared and was replaced by the beaming face of Ray Stubbs. My father showed a turn of pace like that of a young Les Ferdinand as he started powering his way back towards the Hotel California. My brother Rich and I sped off in hot pursuit, desperate to get back to our room and get confirmation from Ceefax. As soon as we reached the hotel, the telly was turned on, BBC 1 was selected, and page 302 was called up: *Shearer signs for hometown club for £15m page 303* read the headline. I sat back on the bed and caught my breath. It was true. Little did I know what contribution Alan Shearer would make over the next ten years.

For me the best thing about having Shearer in the line up didn't relate to goals, it was about having a leader on the front line who would have taken a bullet for the club. I have never seen the stats on front post clearances from opposition corners but I dare to hazard a guess that it is the highest in Premiership history. I should imagine the same goes for winning headers against defenders who are significantly taller than him (I should think if most English football fans were to estimate Alan's height they would place him above six foot, a tape measure and a straight back would suggest different). There was an incident in a game at Charlton Athletic, when times were tough and the younger players were looking to their seniors for guidance. As I remember it, we had already thrown away a lead and were fighting for a point. Charlton won a corner, the ball was whipped in. A Charlton player leapt and attacked the ball. In the melee that followed Al retreated to the goal line. Now we've all seen goal line clearances before, but the leadership shown by our number 9 as he held on to the goal post, hacked the ball clear and then bellowed, 'OUT!' was evident for all to see. It sounds like a small incident, but one appreciated by the Toon Army as much as any 25-yard volley or towering back post header would be. Cheers for the ten years, Al.

Kris Flinn, Newcastle United season ticket holder, Stalybridge, Cheshire

Top ten goals

Alan's best Toon strikes, in chronological order:

1 **Wimbledon**, St James' Park, 21 August 1996
With two minutes left on the clock in his home debut, Alan Shearer stood over a free-kick 25 yards from goal. Few expected anything else than a goal, but the perfect curler into the top corner of the net was a most exquisite start to record haul of goals.

21 **Leicester City**, St James' Park, 2 February 1997
Newcastle were 3-1 down, and a six-man wall plus goalkeeper Kasey Keller stood between ball and net.

But Shearer despatched a ferocious, unstoppable free-kick – the first goal of a determined hat-trick that gave Newcastle a 4-3 win.

52 Tottenham Hotspur, Old Trafford, 11 April 1999
Extra time in the FA Cup semi final, and Shearer had already put his side 1-0 up from the penalty spot. But he secured Newcastle's ticket to Wembley with a 20-yard raker, curled with the outside of his boot past Ian Walker into the corner of the net.

97 Aston Villa, St James' Park, 3 November 2001
Craig Bellamy scored two great goals in this 3-0 win, but they were overshadowed by a fantastic finish from his strike partner. Rob Lee hit a long pass into the penalty area that Shearer met with a sublime inside-of-the-foot volley to beat Peter Schmeichel.

100 Ipswich Town, St James', 27 November 2001
His 99th goal, also scored in this game, was arguably better, but Shearer's 100th strike for Newcastle was worth savouring. Nolberto Solano drove a low ball into the six-yard box, and Shearer arrived to sweep it home to claim a ton of goals for the Toon.

110 Bolton, St James' Park, 2 February 2002
A heroic effort, this one, as Shearer flung himself headfirst through a couple of defenders to meet Aaron Hughes' cross and power it into the back of the net. It was Shearer's second equaliser of the match, and Newcastle won 3-2.

130 Man United, Old Trafford, 23 November 2002
This was blink and you'll miss it stuff, as Shearer hammered an unstoppable 30-yard free kick into the top corner of the Manchester net to draw his side level at 2-2. Newcastle lost the game 5-3, but Shearer's 100th Premiership goal for Newcastle would never be forgotten.

131 Everton, St James' Park, 1 December 2002
Technically the pick of all 206 goals, this was Shearer's own favourite. Shola Ameobi headed a long ball down from the edge of the area, and Shearer connected with an amazing 25-yard dipping volley that flew over Richard Wright into the goal.

173 Chelsea, St James' Park, 25 April 2005
An astonishing long-range winner. Shearer was 30

yards out, with his back to goal, when he received Olivier Bernard's pass. He turned marker Marcel Desailly and lashed a stunning shot across keeper Marco Ambrosio into the far corner of the net.

201 **Portsmouth**, St James' Park, 4 February 2006
This was the goal that saw Shearer overtake Jackie Milburn to become Newcastle United's greatest ever goalscorer. Shearer won the ball in the air, Shola Ameobi flicked it on, then Shearer held off former teammate Andy O'Brien to poke home goal 201.

A true hero

Having been a keen and active follower of Newcastle United Football Club from a young age, I've experienced a fair share of black and white centre-forwards – from good to bad, genius to useless. Since I've just begrudgingly turned 26 years old, some may say that my knowledge is fairly limited but I am well aware of the legacy that the likes of Hughie Gallagher, Wyn Davies, Len White, Malcolm Macdonald and of course the great Jackie Milburn have left.

Yes the Geordies have and always will love their centre forwards and watching an exciting attacking style of football – which has long been at the centre of many debates over the club's long run without success and the defensive frailties that have dogged us for what seems like our entire history.

I, of course, am no different. Born in St Mary's Hospital in 1980, I am as Geordie as the water in the river Tyne. The first football match I went to was Kevin Keegan's testimonial and, being very young, I remember being bemused by the whole thing, wondering if Kevin always left the pitch in a helicopter and whether all football matches were like this.

I quickly learned that they weren't, as I gained my early football education during Newcastle's mid 1980's slump, sitting in a shed in front of the away supporters in the Leazes End. The team was in turmoil, the board was in turmoil but we still turned up as true Newcastle supporters always do.

Looking back, it was a pretty barren time in terms of players to idolise but back then I didn't really care how they played – if they wore black and white then I admired them. I had soft spots for Kevin Brock, David Kelly, Micky Quinn (who can forget his four goals against Leeds?) and of course the illustrious Mirandinha. Being a bit naive in those days, I had a bizarre affection for Kevin Dillon who famously never scored in his time at St James but I just think he was unlucky.

Of course the gloom was quickly lifted with the return of Special K, who restored some pride back into Newcastle's centre forward legacy, namely Andy Cole. But the best was yet to come.

I'll admit it wasn't until he turned out at St James' Park for Blackburn and destroyed us with a man of the match display that I discovered Alan Shearer. I hated him that day.

Much later, I would put myself in Alan's shoes and realise that Alan was only doing his job that day against Newcastle. It summed up two fundamental characteristics that define Alan Shearer – he's incredibly professional and loves scoring goals.

The summer of 1996 seemed to last forever and was one of the best times of my life, I suspect the same was true for Mr Shearer as well. While he was winning the Premiership with Blackburn, picking up the golden boot at the European Championships and signing for a then British record £15million fee to his beloved Newcastle United, I was completing my GCSEs, watching the captivating Euro 96 championships, and winning a gold medal at the Paralympics in Atlanta. Certainly mine and Alan Shearer's lives would never be the same.

I'm not ashamed to say that I was over the moon when Shearer signed, even though I previously disliked him. However, it's the sign of any great sports person that your opponents don't like you, its like a show of respect and Shearer has never been a stranger to opposing fans showing him 'respect' throughout his career.

So I immediately had to have a Newcastle shirt with 'Shearer 9' on the back, but it turned out that lots of other people had the same idea and my Mam queued nearly all night to make sure I had it in time to take to Atlanta. I missed the Charity Shield while I was at the Paralympic holding camp in Pensacola, but I wasn't too bothered as we got beat 4-0 and it poured with rain. When I returned from Atlanta I had my photo taken on the pitch with my Shearer shirt, my gold medal, the main man himself, Kevin Keegan and my then favourite player and friend Pavel Srnicek.

In the build up to the 2000 Sydney Paralympics, the Great Britain team went to the German Championships and it was at the same time as Euro 2000 and England were playing Germany on that weekend. Shearer had announced he would retire from international football after Euro 2000, so I decided to get a shirt to commemorate his England career. It was an England shirt with 'Shearer 9 Forever' on the back. I wore it all the time I was in Germany, drawing many derogatory comments. Those comments turned to sweet silence the next day though, after Shearer sent the Germans packing with a top diving header at the back post.

Later that year, before I went off to Sydney for the Paralympics, Alan presented me with a t-shirt that my parents had got hold of which had 'Miller 1 Forever' printed on it. It was indeed a very humbling gesture.

Without a doubt in my mind, Alan Shearer's best performance in a Newcastle shirt was in the Champions League against Inter Milan at the San Siro, and I was there! Well, I think half of Newcastle was there by the end of the game. The San Siro is the most amazing football ground I have ever been to. It was deserted when we arrived there and in the cold light of day it was most unimpressive. Situated in the barren outskirts of Milan on a big square of concrete, I felt a bit let down. Once inside, the stadium looked more impressive. The huge high stands all around made you feel very enclosed. Once 80,000 fans were inside the atmosphere was electric, and the ground was full an hour before kick off – unheard of in England.

We had tickets with seat numbers on but we quickly learnt that these would be useless and once inside you just had to grab a bit of plastic and either stand or sit on it. People were already standing in the gangways when this guy and his girlfriend came up to me and claimed I was in their seat, I looked at them and laughed, 'You're joking aren't you?' gesturing at all the Geordies just standing anywhere.

Five minutes after kick off and Geordies were still pouring in and it was literally shoulder to shoulder. Just like the good old days. From what I could see of the match, we were playing well and the Italians couldn't cope with Shearer, he was unplayable. I was thinking, if we score now it's gonna be dangerous. Right then, Bellamy skins the full back and squares for Shearer. We're 1-0 up in the San Siro!

Before the ball went in, time seemed to stop, and I lost all sense of sight and sound as 12,000 or so Geordies jumped all over the place. After five minutes of holding tight and trying not to end up down the front, I celebrated the goal. By then it was half time and we could bask for a while in the glory of leading at the San Siro, albeit sitting in a completely different place to the start of the match.

A quick Vieri goal after the break and alarm bells start ringing, but Shearer has them scared stiff and the Internazional defence makes a fudge of a routine cross from Robert and Shearer pounces to regain the lead, this time right in front of the Toon Army. I'm dreaming. Geordies flying over my head again and people are still coming in the stadium, surely not with tickets.

The only sour point was when the animals, also referred to as Inter Milan fans, decided to started throwing objects at the Geordies below, after their side breached our struggling defence to equalise – first they threw lighters, then bottles of water, and then a flare (we just danced round it, nothing they could throw would spoil our day). The guy in front of me stupidly tried to throw coins back at the idiots on the above tier but continually fell short, meaning some poor Newcastle fans were probably wondering how the hell they were getting hit by coins.

A creditable 2-2 draw is what we got out of it but the thousands of Geordies who travelled to the cultural Italian city knew that it was much more than that. They saw one of their own giving a commanding performance on the highest stage of club football, inspiring us to rock one of Europe's greatest footballing stadiums like it's never been rocked before. I'm sure Alan Shearer and everyone of the Toon Army walked out of the San Siro a foot taller that night.

Yes Alan Shearer has done something that is quite rare these days, he has been one of the best footballers in the world for over a decade, his courage, determination and self-belief have been an inspiration and throughout it all he has maintained his dignity. A true hero...

Stephen Miller, Paralympic gold medallist and Newcastle United supporter, Cramlington

Heroes

When I need the strength to carry on
and there's nothing left within,
that's when I look to you.
When I need to know the way to go
and there is no path,
that's when I take your direction.

When I need the inspiration
and have no motivation,
that's when your words mean so much.

When I need a hero
and nobody is here,
that's when you are part of me.

When you are gone
and your legend lives on,
that's when new heroes are born.

Stephen Miller

The Shearer era

I always thought that it would have been great to live through the Milburn era and see him play live in front of me and score goals. However, when you think about it we have been so, so lucky to have been able to live through the era of another legend in Shearer. I have been privileged to follow Shearer's whole career, every game, every goal, watching live games and highlights on TV, even getting goal flashes on mobile phones. Of course, in Milburn's era that wouldn't have been possible as much of the technology wasn't available.

In 50 years there will be young Toon fans saying

how much they would have loved to have been around for the Shearer era, how much they would have loved to see him play, how much they would have loved to witness the admiration that the fans at the time showed Wor Al and how envious they are to have missed out on it. However to all the Shearer fanatics who are reading this, we were here, we got to see it all, every last second of Shearer, every joyous moment, every goal, every celebration, every interview. Simply we got the lot. We should count ourselves extremely lucky that Shearer's Toon career came about when we were alive and I will treasure it, even in 40 years time when I tell my kids all about him. There's no way they will be anything but Toon fans that's for sure, and Shearer is one of the reasons for that. Even in 2050 or any year when I'm old and grey, I'll be getting Shearer's name on my grandchildren's shirts. Retire in peace Mr Shearer, you did good!

Kieran Glennon, Newcastle fan since age of 10, Dublin

Not just any player

Alan Shearer is not just any ex-Newcastle United player. He is, and forever will be, a true legend. He will always have a special place in my heart, and the heart of every other loyal Geordie supporter, because of the amazing ten years of goals and determination he has given us.

Amazingly, he was rejected by Newcastle as a schoolboy, but then in 1996, Alan sensationally 'came home' and became the worlds most expensive footballer, when his boyhood hero, Kevin Keegan, brought him to Newcastle United for £15 million! He followed his heart and turned down years of trophies and success at Man United to join his home town club. A gesture which will live long in the memory of all Newcastle fans, including mine.

He made the decision to retire from international football at the age of 30, to focus on his Newcastle career, and then resisted many calls from England to return.

Although he didn't win any silverware with Newcastle, he has broken many records and gained plenty of awards. Alan has an OBE for his services to Association Football, won many PFA player of the year awards and of course experienced what very few people do, he captained both England and Newcastle United – he 'lived the dream'! He will always be remembered as Newcastle's greatest number 9, due to the fact that he tops the record tables as the all-time leading premiership scorer, with a staggering 260 goals. He is also Newcastle United's top scorer in both league and cup games and in Europe. In the FA cup, he is second, only to the legendary Jackie Milburn.

In England's history books, he is named as joint-fifth all-time leading scorer, with 30 goals. This is an amazing achievement for someone who labelled himself as 'only a sheet metal worker's son from Gosforth'.

In his ten years at Newcastle, he has scored an amazing 206 goals, breaking Jackie Milburn's record of 200. The day that Big Al scored his 201st goal for the club will never be forgotten. The reception the crowd gave him that day lifted the roof off, and will live forever in the Geordie legend's memory. Other goals that will go down as some of his best are the ones against Arsenal in 2000 and Everton in 2002. He has formed some incredible strike partnerships with other incredible players. The ones that I will remember are when he played alongside Les Ferdinand, almost ten years ago and more recently the partnership that he and Michael Owen made this season. I only wish Michael had been able to play more with Alan to relive the famous England years. Alan's very last goal was also very special. Quite typically, it was a penalty and Shearer wasn't going to miss that opportunity, especially against local rivals, Sunderland. This goal came, quite fittingly, in his very last game for the club and in his career. After putting off retirement from the previous year, Shearer had announced he would finish at the end of the 05/06 season. Unfortunately, an injury prematurely ended his illustrious career. This was devastating news for each and every supporter, who had wanted to watch the inspiring number 9 play just a few more times. However, it must have been even more devastating for Alan himself, who knew he would never wear the black and white shirt again.

Throughout his playing career, he has been known as a local hero to so many people and has inspired so many youngsters to follow their dreams, by showing them that through hard work and persistence, you can fulfil them.

Because of his loyalty throughout his unforgettable career, there was one more match for him to take part in – his testimonial. What a night.

The fact that Alan wouldn't be taking a very big part in it – due to injury – was somewhat irrelevant to me. I mean, I was disappointed that he couldn't play, but that didn't stop me making sure I was there to say goodbye for the last time. There was no way I was going to miss seeing Alan Shearer walk out in the famous number 9 shirt for the last time, and the amazing atmosphere of St James' Park on that very special evening. So I was there. I was there, joining in with the chanting and singing, with all the other 52,000 fans who had turned up to pay their respect to their local hero, and to see him put the ball in the back of the net for the very last time. That night was an experience that I for one, will never forget.

That may have been the last time he would walk out at St James' Park as a player, but I knew he would be back in the future, playing a different role at his beloved club. He is admired and adored by thousands and we all expect to see him one day as manager of the club he loves so much.

So when we applauded at the end of his testimonial and Ant and Dec presented him with various awards, we said goodbye to Alan Shearer, centre-forward for Newcastle United, but we all looked positively at his retirement and prepared one day, to welcome back to St James' Park, the legend that is Alan Shearer.

Rachel Armstrong, Newcastle United fan, Hexham

Top ten games

Al's best NUFC matches, in chronological order:

Newcastle 2-0 Wimbledon, 21 August 1996

As home debuts go, this was pretty much perfect. David Batty gave Newcastle the lead after just three minutes with a superb 30-yard lob over goalkeeper Neil Sullivan. United, boasting a forward line of Shearer, Ferdinand, Asprilla and Ginola, easily held onto the advantage. Then, with just two minutes left, Newcastle were awarded a free kick outside of the box. Shearer duly curled the ball over the Wimbledon wall and into the far corner of the net.

Newcastle United 5-0 Man Utd, 20 October 1996

Regarded by many Toon supporters as the greatest Newcastle performance in living memory, few fans will have enjoyed this comprehensive victory as much as Alan Shearer. Newcastle had been whacked 4-0 by the Champions in the season-opening Charity Shield, but revenge was very sweet. Darren Peacock headed the opener, David Ginola blazed in the second, then Shearer set up Les Ferdinand, before scoring one himself. Philippe Albert memorably sealed things at 5-0, but it was Shearer who was the driving force behind a magnificent team performance.

Newcastle 4-3 Leicester City, 2 February 1997

Robbie Elliott gave the Toon a third-minute advantage in this one, but Leicester powered back through Matt Elliott, Steve Claridge and Emile Heskey to lead 3-1 with just 13 minutes left on the clock. Enter Alan Shearer. First the United striker drove in an unstoppable free kick, next he twisted and turned to drive a low shot home, then he tapped in Rob Lee's cross to claim an incredible match-winning hat-trick. In doing so, Shearer offered up a textbook example of a player taking a game by the scruff of the neck.

Newcastle United 1-0 Sheffield Utd, 5 April 1998

An FA Cup semi final at Old Trafford, and more than 20,000 Toon fans enjoyed an unforgettable occasion – thanks to another winning goal from Alan Shearer. Newcastle were favourites, but there was virtually nothing between the two sides until Shearer got his head to a John Barnes cross. Keeper Alan Kelly blocked the header, but the ball bounced onto the goal line. Shearer charged on and poked the ball home. Not the greatest goal of his career, but a priceless one that sent Newcastle to Wembley.

Newcastle United 2-0 Tottenham, 11 April 1999

For a second successive season Newcastle played an FA Cup semi final at Old Trafford, and for the second successive season it was won by Alan Shearer. This one went to extra time, and Shearer was handed the first goal on a plate after a handball in the penalty area by Sol Campbell. But the second goal was a cracker – an unstoppable 20-yard drive that curled away from the keeper into the corner of the net. 'The place was jumping, Shearer cheekily noted. 'I imagine it's been a long time since Old Trafford's been like that!'

Newcastle 8-0 Sheffield Wed, 19 September 1999

Just four weeks previously Shearer had looked to be on his way out of Newcastle after being infamously dropped for a derby match by Ruud Gullit. But now Bobby Robson was in charge, and he was given a fantastic welcome before this match. The restored Shearer hit a twelve-minute hat-trick in the first half, then netted twice more in the second to take his personal tally to five. Aaron Hughes, Kieron Dyer and Gary Speed also scored to complete the rout – Newcastle biggest Premiership victory.

Newcastle 3-1 B. Leverkusen, 26 February 2003

The Champions League is football's toughest club competition, but on this night Alan Shearer made it look easy. He netted a first-half hat-trick against Bayer Leverkusen, scoring two headers and a penalty within little more than 30 minutes. Only a select few strikers (including former Toon star Tino Asprilla) can claim to have performed such a feat at such a high level. As the televised group match continued, Leverkusen missed a penalty, and eventually pulled a goal back through Babic. But United held on for a Shearer-inspired victory.

Inter Milan 2-2 Newcastle United, 11 March 2003
Around 12,000 Newcastle fans travelled to the San
Siro for this huge Champions League clash. United
were on top for much of the game, and Shearer deservedly gave his side the lead just before half-time,
knocking in a Craig Bellamy cross. Christian Vieri
equalised after the restart, but Shearer almost immediately restored the Toon's advantage. Corboda
headed in an Emre cross to make the final score 2-2
– only a draw, but what a draw, as Shearer's name
rang out around one of the most famous football
stages in the world.

Sunderland 1-4 Newcastle United, 17 April 2006
Newcastle were awful in the first half, and went a
goal down to relegated Sunderland through Justin
Hoyte's 32nd minute strike. But Glenn Roeder delivered a stinging half-time reprimand – and it worked.
First Michael Chopra stole in to stab in an equaliser.
Then United were awarded a penalty, and up
stepped Alan Shearer. He had famously missed a
pen against Sunderland in 2000, and the Mackems
had never let him forget it. There was no way he
would miss this one – he successfully despatched it

in classic style. Charles N'Zogbia and Albert Luque completed the rout, but by then their injured skipper had limped from the field. Alan Shearer would never play for Newcastle United again, but what a great way to bow out.

Newcastle United XI 3-2 Celtic, 11 May 2006

Included for what it represented as an occasion, rather than for being a particularly brilliant game, this was much more than a football match. The injured Shearer kicked off, and then left the field, leaving a United side featuring guests Rob Lee, Gary Speed, Les Ferdinand, and Steve Watson to play out a goalless first 60 minutes. Then Albert Luque scored a great volley to give United the lead. However it seemed Celtic hadn't read the script as Maloney and Hartson scored to steal a 2-1 lead. But, in injury time, Ferdinand rattled in an equaliser off a Celtic defender, and then went down to win a penalty. Enter Shearer. He scored, of course. There were songs and scarves, fireworks and flags, and a few tears. An unforgettable end to a magnificent career.

The word is 'legend'

Alan Shearer was a committed, dedicated and loyal footballer. He may not have won many major trophies, but football is not all about how many trophies you can win and what Alan did on the football pitch is unrivalled.

The word legend is bandied about way too much in football these days but Alan Shearer is above that status. I think what makes it even more special is that he is a local boy playing for his hometown club.

There are so many great players about today and there are some truly great players. Shearer turning down Manchester United to join Newcastle shows exactly how loyal he is, lets face it, he would have won everything at Manchester United and I think he knew that, now and then.

We all knew Shearer was something special the day he made is full professional debut, as a teenager, he showed the class and determination that would make him the prolific goalscorer we all know and love today. To score three goals is impressive enough but to do it against Arsenal is spectacular.

It was at Blackburn however when he really showed his class, his superb eye for goal, strong partnership with Chris Sutton and his bravery all combined to help Blackburn win the league in 1995. That is unfortunately Alan's only medal, a man of his stature and quality deserves a lot more.

At Blackburn, Shearer was not only a great goalscorer but he was also quite the goal provider, back in the days when he had pace he would chase down the ball and could produce a deadly cross into the box. I remember one Blackburn fan having once told me 'We need two Shearer's, one to cross the ball, and one to head it'.

The day he joined Newcastle, the scenes that day were stunning, I think it was around 15,000 fans that turned up to welcome him, you would not see that at any other club in the world. Newcastle fans are the most passionate fans and their local hero had come home.

I think the belief at the time was, we can't be stopped, because we had just come second in the league and we all thought that now we had Shearer, the best striker in the world at our club, we have to win the league. It didn't happen, but not that we need to be reminded.

He came home to bring silverware to Newcastle United. He tried and tried and never gave up. His tireless efforts have inspired us through to two FA Cup finals and in his first season, a title battle. It was heart breaking in those two Wembley finals, we went with such hope and belief and came home disappointed. When it really hit hard was seeing Shearer's face at that second final, two consecutive seasons he had scored vital goals to be there and both times it wasn't to be. You could see how hard Shearer was trying to hide his disappointment and congratulate the cup winners, but for a man who has the club in his heart he must have been crying inside.

The goalscoring records he set may never be broken. He currently sits proudly at the top of the list for the all time Premiership goalscorers – he is the only player to surpass the 200 and 250 mark. He is the only player to score 100 for two clubs. He is the all time top goalscorer for Newcastle United FC.

I will never forget that moment he broke the club goal record, he scored a goal at the start of early January to equal it and went on a bit of a goal drought and in those games I sat there with rest of the fans and everyone, every time Shearer touched the ball, was hoping for the goal and waiting for the net to bulge, and then on one day in February it finally did. I remember the song *'If Shearer scores, we're on the pitch'*. The fans were just so passionate.

Shearer also proved his class at international level. It was Graham Taylor who gave him his debut, in the hope that he was good enough to replace the retiring Gary Lineker. He scored in that game, a typical poacher's goal as I remember.

There was certain doubt about him heading into Euro 96 and as ever Shearer answered his critics with five goals to make him the overall top scorer. The goal against the Dutch was a fantastic display of combination play and team work. He was then to be named captain, despite many people believing that Tony Adams should have been given the job. Before retiring he gave us one more thing to cheer about, it didn't keep us in Euro 2000 but one Shearer goal meant that we finally beat the Germans after years of trying.

The thing I admire most about Alan Shearer is the fact that you can't keep him down. Shearer has always been criticised throughout his career but he has answered those critics every time. Every time someone tried to put him down he comes back better than ever. This ability to bounce back has also seen him comeback from some terrible injuries in the past, injuries that end other players' careers.

I would imagine Shearer to be an absolute nightmare for any defender, he is big and strong and you don't want to challenge him in the air unless you're extremely brave because he goes up with his elbows, which we love him for because he is English. He is almost impossible to defend against. He is the complete all round centre forward, he is English and there probably will not be another like Shearer in the next 50 years.

The night of his testimonial, it was phenomenal, 52,000 all-seater stadium completely sold out. Every fan there to cheer on one man, it was almost as if he was a God and he was there to be worshipped. The greeting he got was truly incredible. You try and tell me about a better testimonial, it cannot be done.

The man was above an idol, he is Alan Shearer, he is *our* Alan Shearer.

Barry Worsley, Newcastle fan, Stockport, www.toon-army.co.uk

The reason Alan Shearer has become a legend in Newcastle is down to one word and that word is loyalty – loyalty to the city and loyalty to this city's football club. Over the years fantastic footballers have left the area to play for more prosperous clubs – Gazza, Beardsley and more. But Alan Shearer came at the top of his game, as England No 9 and Captain, and was probably the best out and out centre-forward on the planet at that time, so for him to come home and play for NUFC was just mindblowing. With other top strikers, you know they will probably stay for 2-3 years and they'll be off to another club but with Alan you kind of knew he'd be here for life. He has seen five managers leave in his time at the club, but he has stuck with us, and for that and the quality of his football he will be remembered in this city forever, because in my honest opinion I don't believe Newcastle will ever have a hometown lad give as much to the people of this city.

Ron Bennett, Newcastle season ticket holder, Westerhope, Newcastle upon Tyne

I really fell in love with football when I saw the Newcastle team in the 1996-1997 season, when I was about nine years old, with all those marvellous players: Robert Lee, Les Ferdinand, Pavel Srnicek, Warren Barton, David Ginola and of course Alan Shearer. Why do we love Alan Shearer so much? There is a saying in football that you always notice the strikers, because they are the most spectacular, but that's not all, we love him because he has put his heart and soul into every performance, we love him because he has pushed the squad and served as an inspiration for other players, because he has proved to be a remarkable athlete and a wonderful person, because he has never let us down. Alan Shearer is our pride and joy. He is a football icon, not only for Newcastle or for England, but for the whole world. He is our captain and will continue to hold that place in our hearts even after his retirement. For me, he is the player who has most influenced my life and my views regarding football. He is a legend who deserves a place in any hall of fame.

Alex Calinoiu, Newcastle fan, Romania

I'm a life long Arsenal fan and wish to congratulate Alan Shearer who has been a great football star for club and country. The Premiership will miss him dearly. I have great respect for Alan, who never let his status as a Premiership star go to his head and was a genuine one-of-the-people kind of guy who always had a good thing to say about the Arsenal and I will never forget that. In fact he never had a bad word to say about anyone. I wish him well and hope to see him in the Newcastle dugout one day as manager. As they say, there's no place like home, and St James' Park is his home.

Alan Ryan, Arsenal FC supporter

Wow, thank you for the football memories. I'm not a season ticket holder, I live in Derbyshire, but me and my dad have followed Shearer all the way. What a great role model for football. What a true gentleman he is. So all I can say to sum up is that he is a legend, a true footballer, and a star. Thank you Alan.

Mark Roberts, Newcastle supporter, Derbyshire

Wor Shearer

Awe inspiring skill that you
have proven with the ball,
I've felt the glory so much so
your shirt is on my wall.
We're snapping up your souvenirs
but not to sell on later,
For many made an impact
but your legacy is greater.
Conversation centres round
the goals you have provided,
And bravery with head wounds
from the times you have collided.

I think of Geordie glory
every time I cross the Tyne,
And all the streets are buzzing
thanks to you, our number 9.
Your landmark testimonial
where all those scarves swung free,
And Tyneside still remembers
your award of O.B.E.
Proof is in the Magpies
and the volume that's so loud,
And Jackie Milburn's looking down,
he's smiling and he's proud.
We knew that you'd be special
with the power to astound,
And worth each quid we paid for you
in fifteen million pound.
Penalties and headers
where you really made your mark,
With thanks from all the loyal fans
who fill St. James' Park.
The fast, the bold and beautiful,
our Captain and our pride,
And privileged to see your form
when playing for our side.

Our love for you will never die,
forever to grow dearer,
Behold our golden memories
and thanks to you Wor Shearer.

Christopher Short, Newcastle fan and poet,
Lanchester

Not enough superlatives

I don't think there are enough superlatives to sum up the contributions of Alan Shearer.

He may have ended his Toon career without a medal but could anybody have done more than Shearer to try to make the dream possible? When I look back at the two FA Cup semi-finals against Sheffield United and Tottenham, there was only ever going to be one hero – and both times it was Shearer with his tap-in against the Blades and double against Spurs.

And don't forget he came the width of the post against Arsenal back in the 1998 FA Cup final to possibly turning the game on its head with the Gunners 1-0 up. The reaction of the Toon Army at Wembley had that gone in might have changed the whole course of history, and anybody who remembers the day Rob Lee scored against Chelsea two years later in the semi will know what I am talking about – an equaliser against the Gunners would have set up a deafening finale by the Geordies on a day when United were second best. Everyone has their favourite Shearer goal, the volley against Everton in 2002 in front of the Gallowgate, his howitzer against Chelsea from more or less the same spot in 2004, or what about his unique volley against Aston Villa from an almost impossible angle. His first goal against Wimbledon always sticks out too, it was the start of a love affair really. There are just too many to pick from but for pure emotion record breaking goal number 201 against Pompey had it all. His final goal at Sunderland from the spot at the Stadium of Light wasn't a bad way to sign off, was it?

It isn't just his goals though. Shearer was the first man back to defend a corner on more times than I can remember, and even the world's best defenders would be proud of some his tackles, I remember when Didi Hamman was sent off at Anfield and Shearer played central midfield, he was awesome even though we lost. And how many times did we see Shearer put in a wicked cross that you could have wanted him to be on the end of! Rob Lee's equaliser at Wembley is the perfect example. Shearer also proved there is more than one way to win a game.

I remember the game against Liverpool in 2003 on that bog of a pitch when Shearer ate up the time late on and neither Sami Hyypia or Stephane Henchoz could stop him holding the ball up in trademark fashion next to the corner flag as we held on to win the match 1-0. I think Jermaine Jenas tried the same thing a few minutes afterwards but ended up on his backside straight away. It has been suggested that the number 9 shirt should be retired in his honour, but that would kill the dreams of every young kid that wants to attempt to emulate Shearer in some way.

The future of Newcastle United is a scary prospect without him, which says it all for me.

Lee Ryder, Newcastle Evening Chronicle

Top five clashes

Alan's most memorable black & white battles:

Neil Lennon (Leicester City) 30 April 1998

A goalless draw at Filbert Street became notorious after Shearer was accused of kicking Leicester midfielder Lennon in the face. Rival fans continued to cite the incident as evidence of Shearer's supposedly dirty play in subsequent years, despite the fact that Shearer was found not guilty of misconduct at an FA hearing. Lennon gave evidence on Shearer's behalf, and a three-man FA committee decided that the kick was a 'genuine attempt to free himself'.

Roy Keane (Manchester United) 15 September 2001

Two of the Premiership's toughest warhorses clashed many times, but the most memorable battle was at St James' Park in 2001. Shearer prevented Keane from taking a throw-in, and a frustrated Keane threw the ball at Shearer. The two skippers squared up, Shearer retained control, but Keane snapped and threw a punch. Keane was sent-off. 'Shearer won, hands down,' Keane later said. Newcastle won 4-3, and, of course, Shearer scored the winner.

Justin Whittle (Grimsby Town) 26 September 2005

This Carling Cup game at Blundell Park exploded into life when former soldier Whittle responded to a foul by Shearer – for which Shearer had immediately apologised – by viciously driving his elbow into the Newcastle skipper's face. Severely bloodied, Shearer required three stitches in his lip – and still bears the scar. 'I just wanted to go out there and do him, because he did me,' said Shearer. Instead, he gained suitable revenge by emphatically smashing home the winning goal. After the match Shearer refused to shake Whittle's hand, while Whittle refused Shearer's offer of a little chat in the tunnel.

Uriah Rennie (Referee) 7 August 1999

Aston Villa were the visitors to St James' Park, but ref Rennie took centre stage. He had already shown seven yellow cards when, after 71 minutes, he issued the only red card of Shearer's career – following an innocuous challenge on Ian Taylor. Even Taylor looked amazed at the decision. This was one clash that Shearer could not win – an appeal against the sending-off was turned down – but Rennie was temporarily demoted from the Premier League list at the end of the season due to poor marks from match observers.

Keith Gillespie (Newcastle United) 3 March 1998

Newcastle were enjoying a mid-season jolly in Dublin when Shearer clashed with Northern Ireland winger Keith Gillespie. Gillespie had been flicking bottle tops at his skipper, and Shearer told him, 'Do that one more time and I'll give you a good hiding.' Two minutes later, the bottle-top flicker was lying in a pool of blood. 'We ran out to see Gillespie spark out in the gutter,' reported teammate David Batty. 'There was blood everywhere.'

Our local hero

What can you say about a truly great football legend? 'Big Al' personifies what any footballer should aspire to, courage, passion, honour, determination and a never say die attitude, he is our 'Local Hero'. My only regret is that I have only seen him play for the last four seasons of his career and dearly wished that I had seen him play in his early days with Newcastle, partnering Sir Les and scoring goals for fun at times.

He may not have won any medals or trophies with Newcastle but he will have the admiration and respect of not only the Newcastle fans but from all true football fans across the world who appreciate and recognise a great football legend.

One of my most treasured memories was the day he scored his 201 goal for the club. I think most fans knew it was going to happen that day, we wanted it to happen, we prayed it would happen, and it did. The fans would have sucked the ball into the back of the net, but we didn't need to. He would have scored if ten keepers had been in goal. The fans, the players, anyone associated with Newcastle wanted it for him and he took it in true 'Shearer Style'. I will never forget the way we all cheered, hugged and sang when the ball hit the back of the net and you could tell from Shearer's face, that goal meant more to him than any other, he broke another legend's record, one that many thought would never be broken but who else could have broken it.

I took my 16-year-old son to his testimonial, which we both thought was an unbelievable evening, the singing, the scarves, Celtic fans, everything was perfect, regardless that he didn't play but what a way to end the match, a Shearer penalty with virtually the last kick of the match. It's a story I will be telling the grandchildren for years to come.

After the match, and after I had stopped crying like a baby, (my God it was emotional at the end) my son said, 'That was the best atmosphere I have ever seen and felt at St James' Park, I'm proud to have been here, this will stay with me forever'.

As we were walking out of the ground, under the Milburn stand, there was a fan standing on the stairs with one of the Shearer masks that were given away at the match. He was obviously well under the influence of drink and enjoying himself but all of a sudden the crowd started to chant *'Shearer, Shearer, Shearer'*, pointing the finger salute at him. So if a drunken man, wearing a Shearer mask pretending to be him, can get a crowd to start chanting him, this must give you some idea of what Alan Shearer means to a Newcastle United fan.

So with a tear in my eye and a lump in my throat, thanks 'Big Al', you will be missed but we all hope and pray you'll return some day. This is not the end, just the start of a new chapter for a local hero.

Paul 'Nobby' Clarke, Newcastle United season ticket holder and adopted Geordie, Greenside

A true great

I am glad to say that I met Alan Shearer twice, once at the Chester-le-Street training ground, and once in Malta, and also had a couple of photos taken with him. He has been my third Newcastle hero in my time as a supporter, the others being the great Jackie Milburn, whom I have also met twice at SJP and had photos with, and Supermac Macdonald, whom I never met.

I couldn't have timed my last visit to Newcastle any better than I did, because I was there to watch the home game against Wigan and the demolition of the Mackems at the Stadium of Light. Of course I saw Alan Shearer score his last three competitive goals and 'unfortunately' his last competitive game. But it couldn't have been any better coming against Sunderland.

I think that the best Shearer goal I've seen (on TV, where we watch all Newcastle games live) was against Everton, I believe it was in a 2-1 home win in season 2002-03.

Since Jackie Milburn's record had to be broken, and to be honest I hoped it would never be, I was delighted that it was Shearer who broke it. And now I can't see anyone else breaking it.

I think that Shearer had a great striking partnership with 'Sir' Les Ferdinand and it was a great shame we didn't win the Premier League when so close with them in the side.

Alan Shearer is a Legend because although he has been so successful and on top all throughout his career, he has never stepped out of line and has had never had his name in the papers for the wrong reasons. He has been a model footballer all young hopeful players should copy. A truly great man!

Louis Azzopardi, Newcastle United follower for over 50 years, Rabat in Malta

Gallowgate lad

As Alan Shearer was born exactly one month and one day after me back in the 70s it's fair to say we both qualify as old school Geordie blokes. We probably had very much the same upbringing; playing football at school, playing football after school and playing Subbuteo on the carpet with little squashed players. As the archetypal big daft centre half I reckon I probably played against him at some point in my school days (I would've had him in my pocket easy). By all accounts we both stood in the same part of the ground with the rest of our age group as well, The Gallowgate End.

Now it's been well documented that Alan was a ball boy when Keegan was a player at Newcastle and I'm sure most of his goals will be covered elsewhere in this tribute but I'd like to concentrate on one incident that sticks in my memory and surely cemented his place in the hearts and minds of Geordies everywhere.

We were playing Manchester United at home early in the 2001 season and the atmosphere was absolutely electric. The stands were crackling with tension, as always when we met this mob. This was further exacerbated by the fact that after a slowish start we had moved into top gear, with our new signings Robert and Bellamy in particular, in the ascendancy but we still knew this would be a hard game.

The game was a cracker. We had been 3-1 up at one point, but the Mancs had clawed us back to 3-3, before Alan put us back in front (with a goal that the dubious goals panel subsequently took off him). Not being a team known for our defensive prowess we had been desperately trying to protect the lead as Man United had thrown everything forward.

We had players of the dubious quality of Dabizas, Griffin and Acuna in the first team at the time, all tryers but no real match for the quality of the opposition we were facing that day. The likes of Beckham, Keane and Veron et al were slowly turning the screw and an equaliser was looking inevitable until, with not long left, the ball went out for a Man United throw. Alan, in an effort to give the lads at the back time to regroup wouldn't release it and managed to wind up Roy Keane so much that he threw a punch at him. Most players would have went down clutching their face, the rest would have backed off sharpish, pale and scared, Alan did neither. He stood nose to nose with the alleged hard man and simply stared at him as if to say 'Is that your best?'

Keane did the 'hold me back' routine favoured by all plastic gangsters as he was sent off but Alan, without taking a backward step, simply continued to stare at him until he left the pitch, totally unfazed by his antics or his reputation. Once Keane had gone the fight went out of Man United and the Newcastle lads, inspired by Shearer's commitment and fearlessness, made sure the points came our way.

This incident, to me, summed up Alan Shearer.

The black and white cause was all he cared about and if he wasn't playing he'd have been in the stands next to us shouting abuse at Keane and enjoying his dismissal. Alan Shearer was, is and always will be a Gallowgate lad at heart.

In conclusion I'd just like to say thanks for the memories big lad, enjoy your retirement and get your boy practising his penalties in the back garden!

Andy Rivers, Newcastle United supporter and exiled Geordie, Banbury

Shearer... local hero

Having just watched one of the numerous documentaries on Alan Shearer, and dried my eyes and blown my nose for the umpteenth time, I'm finally coming to terms with the fact that I shall never see the lion of Gosforth pull on his number 9 shirt again. Mark Knopfler should hold his hands up now and confess that he did indeed compose that wonderful piece of music *Local Hero* for the son of a sheet metal worker. As the teams stepped onto the pitch for Alan's well deserved testimonial and *Local Hero* blasted out of the sound system around the ground, the hairs on the back of my neck stood upright.

52,000 Geordies paying homage to a master crafts-man. The ground was a sea of black and white as young and old said thank you to arguably one of the best strikers Newcastle United has ever seen. Shearer's winning spot kick at the Gallowgate End in the final minute of the game was a fitting end to an illustrious career and as he took his lap of honour the supporters were United in expressing their emo-tions. Many cried openly. Some threw their scarf onto the pitch in the hope that Alan would pick it up and take it away with him, everyone applauded. This farewell for me was just as emotional as the night in 1984 when Kevin Keegan was whisked into the Tyneside sky by helicopter.

It's hard to describe the emptiness that I feel since Alan hung up his boots. In many ways his tes-timonial felt like a wake. A good wake don't get me wrong, the testimonial committee deserve medals for organising such a good send off! No, Alan's re-tirement is not just the end of his career as a player, but it is also the end of an era. In many ways Alan epitomised everything that was great about the good old days. As a youngster at Southampton he was made to clean the first team players boots and the changing rooms. He was disciplined and that most certainly helped him become the player that we all worshipped. Young players nowadays have it too easy and that results in a lot of the spoilt brats that we see at our club year after year. Alan respected others but also demanded respect, and he was a born leader. He worked hard on the training ground and was focussed on the job in hand, knowing when to work and when to play, a man's man.

I got to know Alan in 1996. I was Editor of New-castle United fanzine *The Number Nine* and I put in an interview request with the club in the autumn to interview Alan, and I was invited to meet him at the club a week later. The week dragged as I waited to meet the £15 million pound man but eventually the day of the interview arrived. I never suffered from nerves before interviews as I saw it as part of the job putting the fanzine together, but this day was different. As I approached the players entrance I went cold. I took a few deep breaths, composed myself and walked up to the front desk. I was told to wait and that Alan would be a few moments. When he arrived he was dressed casually in a blue Umbro tracksuit and trainers. Once the formalities were out of the way I switched on my tape recorder and started to interview the man that was to surpass

'Wor Jackie' as the clubs leading goalscorer. He certainly had an aura about him. He was quite friendly, but his answers were short and to the point. As we chatted his close friend Rob Lee walked past and joked with him, Shearer's guard dropping a little, but then he focussed again on the job in hand. As the interview drew to a close I asked him if he'd pose with me for a photograph to accompany the piece. He agreed but wouldn't hold the magazine that I had brought along. Perhaps he didn't want to be seen advertising it, I'm not sure, but who cares? As a doorman in Newcastle city centre I used to see Alan out and about on occasions. When I worked at Chase on the Quayside Alan would always have a quick chat on his way in. He was always in control. Unlike other players who you would see rolling around on the floor or downing whisky chasers with pints, Alan would be quite happy to stand in the corner and chat to his close friends and family. He'd pose for every photo and sign every beer mat. He handled the pressures of a night out just as well as he handled his weekly tussles in the Premiership.

I did upset Alan once and for a time I got the feeling that we weren't exactly on the best of terms. His much-publicised fall out with Newcastle Manager

Ruud Gullit led to him being dropped for a derby game versus Sunderland. I was asked for a quote by a local newspaper on the situation at the club, and I said that as a fan I would always back the manager over a player. I felt that Gullit should be given a chance and that Shearer should accept his decision. Hindsight is a wonderful thing and sometimes we can all make mistakes. This was certainly my mistake. We lost the derby game 2-1. Gullit was gone and I had upset the big man. I did not realise that my words had had such a profound effect, but was told by a friend at the club that it had not gone down too well. It was few years later that I plucked up the courage to apologise to Alan when I bumped into him on a night out and he shook my hand and accepted my apology. I was delighted.

Having followed Newcastle United now for 22 years I can honestly say that Alan Shearer has been the best goalscorer that I have seen at St James Park. We will all miss you Alan. You will always be Newcastle and England's Number 1!

Steve Wraith, editor, *Players Incorporated*, www.playersinc.org.uk

What the papers said

The nation's biggest sportswriters on Wor Alan:

In the aftermath of Alan Shearer's retirement, newspaper sports columnists were quick to pay tribute to the man and his career. And they were (almost) united in their fulsome praise. In *The Sunday Times*, **Joe Lovejoy** called Shearer, 'the archetypal British bulldog,' and, 'the best English centre- forward of his era, and maybe of all time.' **Simon Barnes** in *The Times* suggested that the 'extraordinary' Shearer seemed to belong to another age. 'In fact, I am sure I had an Alan Shearer cigarette card when I was a boy,' he wrote. A common theme was that Shearer seemed to be an almost mythical player. **Paul Wilson** in *The Observer* compared him to comic book hero Alf Tupper, Tough of the Track from the *Victor*. Shearer was, Wilson pointed out, a real-life Boy's Own hero. 'Top player, great career, massive loss to Premiership football. And that's not make-believe.' **Patrick Barclay** in *The Sunday Telegraph* lamented Shearer's lack of medals, 'but, like our Matthews and our Finney long ago, he is part of our lives, to be treasured for ever.' *The Telegraph*'s **Henry Winter** praised Shearer for valuing loyalty over money. 'You cannot put a price on being a local hero,' Winter wrote. 'God only knows when Newcastle will see Shearer's like again.' In the Newcastle *Evening Chronicle*, John Gibson called Shearer, 'a man's man – the last of the English bulldog centre-forwards... Bye pal, and thanks, it was great to watch you.' Inevitably, not all columnists were so full of praise. **Lynne Truss**, the author of *Eats, Shoots & Leaves*, described Shearer as, 'a big, waddling, sullen, dirty, immovable and permanently pointing obstacle to beautiful football.' 'I just can't hear the name Alan Shearer without spitting on the floor,' she wrote in the *Observer Sports Monthly*. Her column did not contain punctuation errors. But most writers chose to celebrate the extraordinary career of one of the greatest footballers of all-time, and expressed a genuine sadness that they would never again see him rattle the ball into the back of the net and wheel away in trademark celebration. *The Independent*'s **Simon Turnbull** called Shearer 'the incomparable warhorse' and 'a Toon totem' who 'lived the dream'. 'They think it's Al over,' he wrote. 'It is now.'

No regrets

It's strange to think that a player who was at the absolute heart of Newcastle United Football Club from the moment he signed for a then world record fee on that glorious day in 1996 was essentially absent from his own testimonial ten summers later. The whole night might have been revolved around Alan Shearer, but the game itself went on without the man in whose honour it was being played.

Injury restricted the leading man to a cameo, kicking the match underway and appearing off the bench to rapturous applause in the dying minutes to strike home a penalty (the last kick of the game) which sealed a 3-2 win for the Toon. Of course it was all scripted, the predictable and perfect end to a memorable night.

But no script could have possibly been as perfect as that for Shearer's final competitive game in a black and white shirt.

Time and again in the aftermath of the derby match on 17th April 2006, in which he picked the injury which ended his career, he was asked whether he had any regrets. And time and again he answered, firmly: 'No'.

He didn't regret signing for Newcastle, he didn't regret snubbing Man United twice and leaving Sir Alex Ferguson even redder-faced than normal, he didn't regret the lack of silverware. How could he possibly regret it, as a passionate black-and-white-blooded Geordie who'd not only had the chance to set foot on the St James' Park pitch for the home side but had also gone on to captain the side and set a new goal-scoring record?

And the one real regret he did have from his ten years on Tyneside he had just exorcised.

On 18th November 2000, we were 2-1 down at home to the Mackems with time rapidly running out when referee Graham Poll awarded a penalty. Normally unerring from the spot, Shearer stepped up to strike the ball home – but, to the horror of all those who had been fully expecting to see the net bulge and our number 9 wheel away arm aloft, Thomas Sorensen saved it. Our chance to salvage a point and (more importantly) our pride had gone, and Shearer was inconsolable.

Which is why, five and a half years later at the Stadium of Light, when Charles N'Zogbia was clumsily hauled over in the area by Justin Hoyte with the score at 1-1, Shearer knew he had a chance to put things right. And put things right he did, smashing the ball past Kelvin Davis with what he admitted afterwards was 'frustration and anger'. Cue an ecstatic celebration in front of the jubilant Toon fans, their unbridled joy mirrored in the face of someone who knew – really knew – what it meant to strike a fatal blow against the Great Unwashed on their own turf.

Ten minutes later, following a challenge with Julio Arca, he had to leave the pitch. He knew it, we knew it – it was all over.

But in the post match interviews he couldn't

keep a smirk from crossing his face: 'It was pay-back time. It's been a long time coming and it was nice to get my own back'. Revenge was sweet.

Sweeter than that first ever Newcastle goal against Wimbledon. Sweeter than the stunning strikes against Leicester, Spurs, Aston Villa, Man Utd, Everton, Chelsea... Sweeter even than that re-cord-breaking 201st Toon goal against Portsmouth. The smirk said it all.

So it didn't matter that he would miss the final three games of the season. It didn't matter that he wouldn't get to play a full part in his own testimonial. It didn't even matter about the lack of silverware. His 206th and last goal for the club had come against the Mackems. He'd given the fans what they most wanted, a derby victory. And being a fan him-self, he'd given himself what he most wanted too.

Ben Woolhead, *Black & White & Read All Over*, www.blackandwhiteandreadallover.blogspot.com

Alan Shearer has been at Newcastle United for ten years, and there are many reasons why he is so popular amongst the fans like myself. I have so many great memories of Alan but unfortunately if I wrote down them all, I'd be writing forever! So, I'll just stick to my greatest memories of Alan.

The day he joined us in '96 was one of the greatest days of my life. A lot of people questioned his price tag at the time, but I would have paid double that amount to bring Shearer to our club. The day all the fans went out to welcome Shearer just shows how much it meant to us, you can ask any fan who was there and I can guarantee they'd have missed their wedding day to be there!

One goal that has stuck inside my mind since he scored it was the cracking volley against Everton back on 1 December 2002. The Toffees' keeper stood no chance. But no goal can compare to when he broke Wor Jackie's record. Every single fan inside St James' Park was lucky to witness that goal. I would have sold my arm on eBay to be there.

Craig Howarth, aged 14, Leicester,
www.toon-army.co.uk

There will never be another

Alan Shearer has served Newcastle United now for ten years. Not, unfortunately ten glorious trophy-laden years, but certainly ten exciting, unpredictable and at times unbelievable years. The Shearer era has led to a generation of Toon supporters growing up and only knowing Newcastle have a good team.

By good team, I mean a top-flight side littered with expensive stars, playing in a fantastic stadium in front of sell-out crowds. Many of the late-teen/early twenty-somethings don't know or don't believe the times before this. Instead of constant top flight football and the challenge for Europe and trophies, before the 90s we were a club that yo-yoed between divisions, were often tipped for the FA Cup but not much else. The ground was an old wooden and concrete hovel with thirty-odd thousand fans every week standing in the rain watching free transfers from Hull, Oxford and Blyth trying to overcome the mighty Carlisle, Rotherham and Grimsby.

Then came Keegan the manager and a new generation of fans who only knew the good times. Keegan's reign peaked when he signed the best striker in the world for the biggest fee in the world, and Shearer immediately eclipsed Andy Cole as our best centre-forward of recent times. Cole had been peddled off to the other United known as Manchester, and Shearer was immediately paired up with 'Sir' Les Ferdinand as the strike force that every defence feared.

Over the last few years, St James' Park has seen some of the best forwards around grace the hallowed turf. Cole, Beardsley, Ferdinand, Bellamy, Ferguson, Kluivert and now Owen reads like a who's who of top forwards, but Shearer is still the king. He had everything the modern striker needed and a ferocious loyalty to his home club.

His greatest asset has probably been his power. Physical strength allied to a bullet shot has characterised his game down through the years. Who can forget such wonder strikes as these? The volley against Everton which turned the game and almost broke the net at The Gallowgate. The shot against Chelsea when Shearer turned Desailley and hit the top corner. The strike against Man Utd at Old Trafford which Barthez couldn't even get close to. The list for Newcastle, Blackburn, Southampton and England is endless.

How about his dead ball kicks? Big Al's first goal for Newcastle was a superb curling shot into the top of the Wimbledon net. Remember the pile-driver straight down the centre of the Leicester goal which led to a great come back and a hat-trick for the great man? Then there was the free kick against Sunderland which sealed another derby victory. Finally, despite a few misses, who would you really want to take a last minute penalty to save the game?

A great strength as well is his heading ability and the way he gets ahead of defenders to power a header into the goal. Always a threat at corners and whipped in free kicks, Shearer was a danger to every team, domestic and international, in the air.

Something that isn't always mentioned, but was a strength of the big man, was his crossing ability. He has always delivered a great ball from the flanks, most noticeably for Ferdinand to score against Man Utd in the 5-0 romp and for Lee to score against Chelsea at Wembley.

Shearer also had the great ability all strikers have – the knack of being in the right place at the right time. There was always a chance Shearer would pop up at the back post, or six yards out to knock in a rebound or tap in a cross. That is some-thing you just can't teach.

No trophies, but ten years of service and over 200 goals means that Alan Shearer is now up there with the legendary forwards in the clubs history. Gallacher, Milburn, Macdonald and now Shearer. There may be other number 9s, but there will never be another Alan Shearer.

Barry Hindmarch, lifelong NUFC supporter, Gateshead

...and the rest

The goals that _don't_ count towards the record:

Only 10,069 spectators saw Alan Shearer's first ever goal for Newcastle United – a penalty in a friendly match at Lincoln City in 1996. 52,275 saw his last – another penalty in his St James' Park testimonial against Celtic in 2006. But neither of these strikes count toward his official goal tally. Alan scored 23 'unofficial' goals in friendlies, plus a penalty shoot out goal against Blackburn in the league cup in 1998. So, while Alan's official goal tally for Newcastle is 206, his unofficial tally is actually 230:

1	09/08/1996	FRE	Lincoln City	A	2-0
2	02/08/1998	FRE	Middlesbrough	A	1-1
3	02/08/1998	FRE	Middlesbrough	H	1-1
4	05/08/1998	FRE	Bray Wanderers	A	6-0
5	05/08/1998	FRE	Bray Wanderers	A	6-0
6	05/08/1998	FRE	Bray Wanderers	A	6-0
7	11/11/1998	PSO	Blackburn Rovers	H	1-1
8	16/07/1999	FRE	SV Deurne	A	4-0
9	31/07/1999	FRE	VFL Bochum	A	2-3
10	31/07/1999	FRE	VFL Bochum	A	2-3
11	13/08/2000	FRE	Espanyol	A	1-2
12	22/07/2002	FRE	Tubanters	A	9-0
13	22/07/2002	FRE	Tubanters	A	9-0
14	22/07/2002	FRE	Tubanters	A	9-0
15	26/07/2002	FRE	UDI '19	A	5-0
16	09/08/2002	FRE	Gateshead	A	8-0
17	09/08/2002	FRE	Gateshead	A	8-0
18	24/07/2003	FRE	Birmingham City	A	2-1
19	01/08/2003	FRE	Hartlepool United	A	6-0
20	01/08/2003	FRE	Hartlepool United	A	6-0
21	01/08/2003	FRE	Hartlepool United	A	6-0
22	05/08/2003	FRE	Bayern Munich	H	2-2
23	05/08/2003	FRE	Bayern Munich	H	2-2
24	11/05/2006	FRE	Celtic	H	3-2

20 questions

Take the following quiz to find out if you are an Alan Shearer superfan. Answers on page 182.

1. Which nation won the World Cup in the year of Alan's birth?

2. Against which team did Alan score a hat-trick on his professional debut?

3. What was the name of the scout that recommended Alan to Southampton?

4. Who played alongside Alan to make up Blackburn's famous 'SAS' strike partnership?

5. Against which nation did Alan score on his England debut?

6. How many goals did Alan score to win the Golden Boot at Euro 96?

7. Against which team did Alan score his only international hat-trick?

8. Alan scored his last international goal for England against which team?

9. Who succeeded Alan as England football captain?

10. What is Alan's dad called?

11. Which team did Alan score against on his Newcastle home debut?

12. How many times did Alan play at Wembley for Newcastle United?

13. How many hat-tricks did Alan score for Newcastle?

14. Who was the only referee to send Alan off?

15. How many penalties did Alan score for United?

16. Which three feature films has Alan 'starred' in?

17. Why was Alan nicknamed 'Smokey' as a youngster?

18. How many goals did Alan score for Newcastle in the Champions League?

19. Which sports company manufactured Alan's boots?

20. Which Tyneside art sculpture was kitted out in a giant 'Shearer 9' shirt in 1998?

Answers over the page...

Answers:

1. *Brazil (1970)*	2. *Arsenal (1988)*
3. *Jack Hixon*	4. *Chris Sutton*
5. *France (1992)*	6. *Five*
7. *Luxembourg (1999)*	8. *Romania (2000)*
9. *David Beckham*	10. *Alan Shearer*

11. *Wimbledon*

12. *Four (Charity Shield 1996, FA Cup Finals 1998 & 1999, FA Cup Semi Final 2000)*

13. *Four (1997 vs Leicester, 1999 vs Sheffield Wed, 2003 vs Bayer Leverkusen, 2004 vs H Sakhnin)*

14. *Uriah Rennie (1999)*   15. *46*

16. *The Match (1999), Purely Belter (2000), and Goal! (2005)*

17. *He loved smokey bacon crisps.*

18. *Seven*   19. *Umbro*

20. *The Angel of the North*

Superfan rating:

0 to 5	Missed the target
6 to 10	Decent effort
11 to 15	Solid performance
16 to 20	Top scorer – Alan Shearer superfan

So you think you're an Alan Shearer superfan?

Then enter this contest. One lucky winner will get a fantastic Alan Shearer testimonial goody bag, and four runners up will receive Tonto Press books.

To enter, simply answer the following question:

Which goalkeeper conceded Alan Shearer's 206th Newcastle United goal?

Send your answer along with your name and address via email to shearer@tontopress.com.

The closing date for entries is 31 January 2007.

Get more details at www.tontopress.com/shearer.

So you think you're an alan Shearer out there?

Supporting the NSPCC

The NSPCC is the UK's leading charity specialising in child protection and the prevention of cruelty to children. In the North East the NSPCC runs four fantastic projects for children and young people.

In Newcastle, at Brighton Grove, we offer a therapeutic service for children who are 'looked after' and have been abused. This involves the use of family therapy, direct and indirect play therapy and counselling. The team works with children aged 4 to 18 and also supports their carers.

In Sunderland our Kaleidoscope project works with children and young people who display sexually harmful behaviour. The aim is to try and understand and change their behaviour and to support their families. The team carries out one-to-one work as well as family and group work.

The North East Specialist Investigation Service, based in Jesmond, is one of a network of independent teams. They work in partnership with police, social services and other statutory child care agencies, primarily to investigate organised, institutional and professional abuse.

Our schools team based in Blyth works in a number of schools in Northumberland offering one-to-one consultations and group work with children.

As well as our local projects, the NSPCC Child Protection Helpline is another vital service helping keep children safe in the North East. The Helpline provides free advice, counselling and information to anyone who thinks that a child may be at risk.

For further information on how you can help support the work of the NSPCC please contact the appeals team on 0113 2299 313.

NSPCC

Cruelty to children must stop. FULL STOP.

tonto press

Tonto Press is an independent publisher based in Newcastle upon Tyne dedicated to developing and supporting new writing.

You can find out more about Tonto Press books and projects at the website: www.tontopress.com

Read more from Tonto Press:

The Unofficial Football World Championships:
An Alternative Soccer History
by Paul Brown
Tonto Sport 2006
ISBN 0955218314, paperback, 192pp, £9.99

We all love the official World Cup, but it only comes around every four years... Welcome to the unofficial alternative.

What if football's world championships pitched teams into a continuous series of boxing-style title matches running way back to the very first international game in 1872? That's the idea behind the Unofficial Football World Championships (UFWC) - probably the least-known but most exciting football competition on Earth.

The UFWC title has been contested by almost 100 nations at more than 800 matches spanning over 130 years. Its amazing story involves legendary teams and footballing minnows, classic finals and forgotten friendlies, and celebrated players and unsung heroes.

This official guide to the UFWC is packed full of classic matches, key players, and fascinating statistics. Irreverent and entertaining, it adds up to an alternative soccer history - and represents a fresh perspective on the most beloved sport in the world.

Available from bookshops and www.tontopress.com

Read more from Tonto Press:

The Burglar's Dog Alternative Guide to Drinking in Newcastle upon Tyne
By Mark Jones
Tonto Press 2006
Coming November 2006

A hilarious and irreverent pub crawl through Newcastle upon Tyne - officially the eighth best party city in the world!

Meet the Burglar's Dog. He's angry and rude, he's got four legs and an abysmal hangover. His essential guide to drinking in Newcastle contains bleary-eyed reviews of more than 140 of the city's best and worst pubs, plus furry-tongued features on how to get the most out of stag and hen weekends and more.

Devastatingly honest, the Burglar's Dog tells it like it is: no gripe is too petty, no insult is too extreme. Essential reading for anyone who has yet to find something even remotely 'to die for' behind the façade of a luxury lounge bar.

Available soon from bookshops and www.tontopress.com

Read more from Tonto Press:

Dial M For Monkey
by Adam Maxwell
Tonto Press 2006
ISBN 0955218322, paperback, 124 pp, £7.99

Adam Maxwell's first collection of short stories is inventive, funny, dark, and hugely entertaining. The twenty stories included here range from a bizarre quest to find a dead rockstar's limb (Jim Morrison's Leg) to a memorable warning about the hidden dangers of building sites (the acclaimed Shooting Jelly With A Shotgun). Effortlessly fusing pop culture, gunplay, and simians, Dial M For Monkey contains a vibrant mixture of short stories.

Tonto Short Stories
Edited by Paul Brown and Stuart Wheatman
Tonto Press 2006
ISBN 0955218306, paperback, 224 pp, £9.99

Tonto Press launches its search for new writing talent with an anthology of twenty fresh stories by twenty exciting writers. Eclectic, absorbing, affecting, and memorable, this page-turning collection represents the very best of short but sweet original fiction. 'Book of the Month' – The Crack. 'To say that English writers don't take risks is stuff and nonsense, as this collection proves' – San Diego Union-Tribune.

Available from bookshops and www.tontopress.com